HINDU LIFE AND CUSTOMS

HINDU LIFE AND CUSTOMS

HELEN CAMERON GORDON

Hindu Life and Customs

ISBN : 978-81-8205-488-2

Reprinted in 2009 in India by
Isha Books
B-63, 1st Floor
New Gupta Colony,
Near DDA Market,
Delhi - 110009
First Published in 1935
Original Title: The Sunwheel- Hindu Life and Customs

Printed at : Vishal Kaushik Printers, Delhi

CONTENTS

PART I

PLATEAU, PLAINS AND HILLS

PART II

HINDU TEMPLES AND THEIR GODS

PART III

HINDU STATES AND THEIR RULERS

LIST OF ILLUSTRATIONS

MAPS

PART I

PLATEAU, PLAINS AND HILLS

ARJUNA
driving the CHARIOT of the SUN

CHAPTER I

LAKSHMI

Queen of the gods, she leapt to land
A lotus in her perfect hand;
And fondly, off the lotus sprung
To lotus-bearing Vishnu clung.
Her, gods above and men below
As beauty's queen and fortune know.

B. A. GUPTE.

It must have been Lakshmi, ocean-born goddess of prosperity and happiness, that brought me overseas from the dark days of an English winter to revel in the sunshine of Mysore State. Under her "auspicious" guidance I came first to Bangalore, the city of the Bean, arriving by rail in six and a half hours from Madras, on an evening of October, that is most sacred to herself.

Had I been Hindu, I must have fasted the day long in preparation for her festival and throughout the dusty, somewhat dull journey over the low-lying plain to this delightful plateau, 3,000 feet above sea level.

The harvest has just been gathered in and from the rising of the full moon of this month, Asvina, the new grain may be eaten with thankfulness and rejoicing. Though Heaven's silver lamp floods the world of India with a tropical radiance, a light should burn outside the house this night, that Lakshmi, wife of the great god, Vishnu, the Preserver of Life, shall stay her steps awhile to bless the inmates.

In the room set apart for worship, an altar has been prepared with her image set in the midst of such other gods as the household may choose to honour, and flowers and fruit have been offered with repeated mutterings of prayers. Afterwards a feast is spread and as sleep is forbidden to all on such a great occasion (lest this grave discourtesy anger the goddess, when she is abroad in the world), the men play at dice, the great game of chance and luck. At midnight the milk of the green coconut is served, emblematic of fertility, that the earth shall again bring forth her increase in due season. Before another harvest festival Lakshmi shall shower wealth upon her devotees.

Yet, there may be others of my Indian neighbours, who may prefer to lay black offerings at the shrine of the goddess of adversity, on the principle, that it is wise "to pay reverence once to a benign god, for he may perhaps do you good, but better pay reverence twice to a malign god, that he may not harm you." However, these victims of fear must be few and far between if they will only bear in mind the legend of a certain king and take their courage in both hands. He had been an unhappy king and his fortunes always under a cloud, whilst he kept on an altar of his palace an image of Bad Luck. At length, the persistence of his wife's worship of Lakshmi every harvest moon, prevailed over his misfortunes and the iron image melted away in the sunshine of felicity.

For me, the night passed in dreamless slumber: the sun had long crossed the border of darkness and was high in the heavens, when I wakened to this strange, unfathomable, age-old world of India. At first this strangeness is unseen, unfelt, for nowhere else than in India is it more possible for the European to live a life of splendid isolation from the people of the country, except for the deft-handed, soft-footed servants, who anticipate one's every want.

In Bangalore Cantonment, replete with the comforts of modern sanitation; water laid on to all bathrooms with fitted basins; electric light and power; fans and frigidaires; English friends exclusively to lunch and dinner; bridge in the late afternoons; dancing, theatricals and cinemas at night, I might be living in some large English country town. Day after day might pass without the slightest revelation of the web of Brahminism, in which the Hindu is enmeshed; of Muslim traditions and ceremonies that have assimilated practices and superstitions of the prevailing creed; of the customs that are founded on the solar myth; on nature and animistic worship, that had their origins at least three thousand years ago.

Life for me had been thus unheeding, when I first came to Bangalore, in my girlhood. To be sure, in those days, we had no Indian neighbours in the British Civil and Military Station, and I never met, nor thought of visiting, a high caste Hindu lady, nor any Muslims—always prisoners in their homes—nor even Parsees, who were noted for their foreign education and intellectual attainments.

Equally unknown to us was the large body of settlers in the suburbs of St. John's Hill, then called "Eurasians," but now designated "Anglo-Indians"—a term which in past days did not imply a mixture of blood, but a European the greater part of whose life, for service or on business, had been spent in India. It is they, the Anglo-Indians of this generation, who are already the greatest sufferers by reason of the movement and change inaugurated by Mr. Montagu. They have occupied subordinate positions in the Government as railway officials and clerks; in Post Offices and banks, and have been insistent—perhaps unwisely—on the British side of their nationality. Now they are told frankly, it is to " Mother India " they must turn for help and protection, whilst being slowly elbowed out of their positions. "Who will watch your interest?" said Sir Henry Gidney on the 10th December, 1934. "If you say that our representatives in the legislatures will do it, you will be living in a fool's paradise." [1] He asked them to identify themselves completely with Indians.

Other terms that have fallen into disrepute are "native" for the Indian, and "*pariah*," for which "*Dravida*" (aboriginal) has been substituted. Lastly, the "Out-

[1] *The Indian Review*, January, 1935.

caste," or "Untouchable" has been rechristened "*Harijan*" in the notorious collection campaign, which Gandhi has carried on, ostensibly for their social and moral uplift.

In Bangalore there are other and more noticeable changes than these subtle distinctions. An increased population has necessitated building operations on a large scale and the compounds of my youthful days have been divided up, that two or three small bungalows may be placed close together within the same area. Yet the number of British and Indian regiments has materially diminished, and in January, 1935, began the Indianization of the Artillery and consequent unemployment of the Indian servant class. As the houses in Cantonment empty of their British tenants, they are occupied by Indians, and the bungalow I lived in, when a girl, has been bought recently for the newly married son of the Dewan, the Maharajah's Muhammedan prime minister, who is already a large landowner in British Bangalore.

More than a century ago, this portion of the City was handed over to the British, that they should administer it under a Resident and continue their protection of the Hindu rulers to whom they had restored Mysore State after the Muslim conquest, ensuring for them the peace and prosperity they have enjoyed ever since. Strategically, it is the most suitable spot for troops in all South India and the British have made of this Civil and Military Station a fine garrison town, with wide roads and excellent shops that supply, not only the necessities, but also the luxuries of civilized life.

There is a large Indian *bazar* with Hindu temples and Muhammedan mosques wedged in amongst a multitude of shops, more or less resembling big cupboards, in streets packed with a vivacious crowd, many-tongued and colourful. In the environs of Cantonment is a model village, built on Indian lines, where the people can live decent, cleanly lives (if they will) in low-rented dwellings, free from the haunting dread of demons and disease. Some are slowly learning that cleanliness will do more

LAKSHMI

for them than propitiation of the seven female deities, who symbolize cholera, swollen necks, coughs, measles and small-pox, all enshrined in company on the outskirts of Bangalore City.

Well do I remember a terrible outbreak of bubonic plague and the difficulties experienced by Authority with regard to inoculation, when a rumour was spread that this was a scheme by means of which Queen Victoria hoped to prolong her own life! The probable victims put greater faith in their worship of the Plague Goddess, whose shrine is in the village adjacent to the Maharajah's Palace, a modernized adaptation of Windsor Castle. The present ruler rarely comes to Bangalore and he is represented by his brother, the Yuveraj, who generally makes it his home and whose son is the next heir. He is called Jaya,[1] for he was born when the guns were announcing the victory of the Allies in the Great War.

There are other important buildings just outside Cantonment, in the beautiful park which is named from a former Resident, Sir Mark Cubbon. Here are a large circular Public Library, a Museum and two great blocks of Public Offices, now supplemented on High Ground by a third. They are the colour of the warm, red earth, that lends much beauty to the landscape. Before the days of motor-cars and tarred roads, the whole Station was often enveloped in a haze: and still, under a radiant sky veiled with filmy particles, the atmosphere has a character and loveliness all its own.

The varying greens of the splendid trees are the more vivid against this colourful, painters' background. They spread a luxuriant shade around large tanks, over grassy slopes and shelter a long avenue near the tennis courts in the park, where Indians have learned to play, with enthusiasm, an English game.

Always a much sought-after Station, Bangalore has now become a favourite place of residence for many who have served India, whose day's work is over and who love the sun. If they leave, for any reason, the

[1] Jaya = victory.

climate lures them back. For ten months of the year it is as perfect as can be any climate on earth, and with electric fans and other amenities of life, March and April, when the temperature is highest, are not too unbearable.

What an enchantment to wake every morning of November and be greeted by the sun, "the great magician whose appearance will transfigure everything," even the colour of one's thoughts. What a delight to look out from the verandah at a wealth of creepers climbing walls and pergolas and high tree trunks to cover them in masses of pink and purple bougainvillea; royal blue, or mauve "morning glory"; waxen blooms that are red-orange; sprays reminiscent of laburnum flowers that have forsaken canary yellow for a lilac hue. Their hanging, many-petalled branches stretch out as if they would shield the poinsettia tree from the hot rays that are fading its leaves from deep crimson to palest pink.

The Brahmin, in the midst of his toilet preparations for the day, bows to the blessed sun and offers an oblation of rice that he may procure favours from the Supreme Person. "Let us meditate," he prays, "on the most excellent light of the Creator; may he guide our intellects." [1]

"To him, whose shape is inconceivable and unmanifested, who is unaffected by the qualities, whose nature is quality, whose form is the support of the entire creation—to Brahma, be homage." [1]

As the hours pass and the sun advances in the heavens, the refreshing shade of the *peepal* tree is flung over the bungalow. It is sacred, for at its root Brahma lives, Vishnu is in its stem and Siva, third person of the Hindu Trinity representing the forces of nature, is at the top. During the "auspicious" month, that falls in our April, the tree must be watered daily. This is a religious duty and always there will be found some pious soul to fulfil it, should it have grown to beautify an isolated spot. But this will be a most pleasant place and the murmur of

[1] *Surya-Siddhânta.*

light breezes rustling through the leaves, to the weary traveller who seeks its shade, is like the ripple of cool waters.

If a Hindu woman has a secret wish—that a son be given to her—she must watch out for the new moon to fall on a Monday, in this same month of April sacred to the *peepal.* She will visit the tree, clad in silk attire, finger on lips, place fruit and flowers at its foot and pass round the trunk one hundred and eight times in silence. If she be rich, her offerings will be of gold, or jewels, that will subsequently enrich the temple priests, and perhaps she may be granted her heart's desire.

It has been said that "all religions are therapies for the sorrows and disorders of the soul," but in South India the creed is composite, dating back in part to the Stone Age. It simply bristles with fears, bogeys, superstitions and malevolent deities, of which there are, literally, millions. Bound up with Brahminism are social laws to be observed from the cradle to the grave, that provide sufficient occupation for every "twice-born" individual to the exclusion of all other work, or recreation. Life for a high-caste Hindu is somewhat overcrowded with important ceremonies; domestic, public and private. Only the most holy, the *Sadhus*, are absolved from the performance of such caste observances, for they have separated themselves from all mundane affairs and pursue their narrow way to divinity, begging-bowl in hand.

For the average man, his religious duty is part of the social framework, which he must perforce uphold, that it shall be maintained intact according to Brahminical Law. Here is indeed a web, in which the weavers are themselves held fast with threads of steel drawn from the ancient writings, or from religious teachers, so that the warp and the woof of it is a mass of unbreakable, current prejudices that date from the beginning of Time.

A death ceremony is held to be of supreme importance to the soul and ample provision must be made for its passage: food cooked for oblations: clothes given in charity, or some equivalent. The disembodied spirit hovers above the mourners for perhaps twelve days and until a crow is found to eat a ball of rice. Only a son can achieve the gift of immortality for his father, whom he delivers from hell by the ceremonies he performs. "There is no heaven for a sonless man." "Even the beasts of the field know that the creature, who does not beget offspring, has no place in the world."[1] Nor is this all. While a son lives, he must perform *shradha* on every anniversary of his father's death.

> Oh my father, my grandfather, my great grandfather!
> Are you satisfied? Are you satisfied?—We are satisfied.

is a necessary formula that occurs in the ritual.

If the son of the house be a cultivator, no animal must work on that day, lest the soul be reincarnated in any one of them. Rebirth in a lower form of life is a punishment for sin.

Of these customs I had some account from a visitor, an Indian Government clerk, now retired, of the Mysore State. In the course of our conversation, he pulled out his notebook, in which he had neatly entered six dates of the deaths of his relatives, for whose *shradha* he is responsible, including his father, his wife and also his mother-in-law. Her children had been daughters only and he was obliged by his marriage to fulfil towards her the duties of a son. Any of these ceremonies would cost him more than he could well afford in food and gifts to the priests and in the entertainment of relatives. "It is through the Brahmins that the spirits of the dead and the gods become pleased"—"A Brahmin is the lord of all created things."[2]

Moreover, in the printed calendar of the notebook might be found three groups of three days each, that are set apart for worship of dead ancestors.

My visitor was rather surprised when I produced a notebook similar to his, in which I had marked the principal Hindu and Muslim fasts and feasts throughout

[1] *The Rites of the Twice-Born.* [2] *Laws of Manu*, I, 99–100.

the year. The Muhammedans, having only one God and a Prophet, do not indulge in many ceremonials, but the list of Hindu festivals is simply staggering. "The whole year," wrote a former Indian Minister of Education, "is full of festivals supposed to commemorate some legendary, or mythological, person: business and work are seriously impeded by the fortuitous occurrence of these interruptions."[1]

My calendar had been given to me by an astrologer; a *pundit* so learned in the courses of the stars, that he had predicted another world war, as the result of the strange phenomenon witnessed at Tokyo, when "the Moon swallowed up Venus." His profession is held in great repute all over India, where it is usual to study the position of the planets before taking a long journey, building a house, buying bullocks, or settling a business transaction.

The astrologer plays an important part in all Indian domestic affairs. It is he who fixes the day and hour that a marriage shall take place and heaven help the poor little bride if, for any reason, her wedding should be postponed to some "inauspicious" moment and she become a widow, cursed by the gods.

When a child is born, its horoscope must be cast at once and the astrologer is summoned. One father learnt, with horror, that this new son of his would be instrumental in causing his own death. Panic-stricken, he murdered the infant, and consequently had to suffer the extreme penalty, as had been foretold. It is said that, by Indians, horoscopes are held to be the equivalent of certificates of birth and that they are so accepted by Insurance Companies. However, in a recent case of abduction, the judge refused to consider the girl's horoscope as legal evidence of her age.

Death, too, is predicted by the conjunction of certain inimical planets, and some two years or so ago, a very great lady fell sick. Her family astrologer bade her prepare for her passing, for it had been written in the

[1] R. P. Paranjpye, M.A., D.Sc.

stars that she must shortly die. It seemed as if it must be so and she sent for an English friend to bid her farewell for ever.

"What nonsense is this?" said the unbeliever in astrological predictions—"Die! Not at all! You are certainly not going to die. Put the idea out of your head at once!" Together, they fought the stars quite successfully, and the great lady has only recently passed on to the other side.

The intimacy which could bring about such whole-hearted co-operation is difficult, and even impossible, for a stranger to achieve: it must be a matter of many years. During my brief visit I have met several Indian ladies and have received invitations to their homes, but never in the mixed social life of men and women to which we are accustomed.

The *Dewan* gave an official garden party to meet distinguished visitors to Mysore and I found a large gathering in the grounds that surround his beautiful bungalow overlooking the race-course. We were received first by his son, who is his private secretary, then by the host himself, and I found myself in company of various nationalities, and many European women. The tennis courts were all occupied and Indian gentlemen were the partners of English girls.

Where, then, was our hostess? I had met her at the Indian Ladies' Club and found her charming to look at and interesting to talk to in my own tongue. It was a disappointment to be told that none of the ladies of the household would appear: they are Muhammedans and still "behind the curtain." How difficult under such circumstances to carry on normal social intercourse.

The great Muslim fast of Ramazan, which fell in the dark half of the sun's year, had just come to its long drawn-out conclusion, and three days previously I had made a tour of the mosques in the *bazar*. They have no special characteristics here and are merely pillared halls with a wide frontage to a courtyard, where water for ablutions is always to be found.

Before entering, I had stood on the threshold awaiting the soft loose slippers, usually provided in Muslim lands, to thrust over one's own shoes for the better preservation of fine carpets. They were non-existent. The Muhammedan in India has become infected with the Hindu caste superstition, that leather—the skin of a dead animal—is impure and brings pollution to mosque, or temple: bare, or stockinged feet are imperative if one would enter even the vestibule of any shrine. Skinning and tanning are noisome occupations and all leather workers are outcasts. To strike a man with a slipper is an unforgivable insult, punishable by law, if taken into Court. However, the case of the *mahout*, who was severely beaten with shoes for having stolen our lord the elephant's flap-jack for his own supper, was probably not one for appeal.

My visits to the mosques had been in company with a Muslim gentleman, who acted as guide and to whose bungalow I went for tea after sundown. It happened to be the twenty-seventh night of Ramazan, the Night of Destiny, when the fate of every man is written down for one year by the Moving Finger, and an especial occasion for Muhammedan hospitality. The ladies of the establishment were all in the kitchen, baking cakes and sending them away, piled up in baskets, to their friends, to be eaten after the prayers of midnight and next morning, first day of a New Year.

My courteous host, who had fed me on sweet cakes till I could eat no more of them, wished to extend his hospitality to the chauffeur, when I was leaving, but he happened to be a Brahmin. Were he starving, he could not accept food from a Muhammedan, nor even from an Hindu except he be of his own, or better, caste. His rice is never boiled, but exposed for two days in the sun, before it is eaten, and is crushed by women with heavy wooden pestles, shod with iron, in a stone or rock hole. He may not eat bread made with yeast, nor baked except by a man of his own caste; and only of late years has it been established "that neither ice nor soda-water count as water for the purpose of conveying pollution."

The next invitation that I received was to the house of a Hindu judge, where the furnishings of the room, and all the appointments of a dainty afternoon tea were entirely English. Afterwards we had excellent bridge, and I might almost have imagined myself in a London drawing-room. In a show cabinet near where I was sitting, I could see an array of silver cups won by the absent master of the house in tennis tournaments. His wife opened the glass doors for a closer inspection of the trophies, pronouncing the winner of them as a "steady, but not a dashing player."

There were other ornaments of her own country, and the invariable wedding present of a silver coconut, emblem of fertility; a hope that the couple may have a numerous family. "The whole of the Indian family story," says Sir George McMunn, "is based on the inseparable bond between husband and wife . . . the joyful duties of procreation." [1] To serve her lord in life is the prescribed religion of every Hindu woman, no matter what manner of husband he may be; nor in death would they be divided, if he should die first, had not the more humane and civilized West said "Nay" to *Sati*.

As the afternoon drew in, electric light illuminated the bridge table, but through the open door I could see the same servant, who had pressed the push-button in the modern way, busying himself on the threshold of the house with a number of tiny oil lamps. These he placed in niches, provided for the purpose and on either side of the entrance, where they could only make darkness visible. Did their feeble flickerings serve to keep out the demons, or were they intended to attract the spirits of ancestors, or even Lakshmi, divine goddess, who draws forth all kindly qualities of the human heart?

On the threshold itself, just within the doorway, was the geometrical figure which is freshly drawn each

[1] *The Underworld of India.*

morning in her honour, in dots, with white clay. It is called "The Salutation of the Threshold." As I was much interested in this drawing, my hostess offered to lend me a book full of different designs for daily use; much as I might have given an Englishwoman a fashion paper with patterns for embroidery, or lace.

Some of them I found too difficult for so poor a draughtsman as I, such as a pineapple, or an elephant; but I learnt that it is important to draw a weird, small device outside the essential figure to ward off the evil eye from the Salutation itself.

We met again, a few days later, at the Indian Ladies' Club, a social idea that under British auspices has developed more rapidly in India than on the Continent of Europe, where it is viewed with disfavour and suspicion by the men. To be sure, in this country no man could be admitted upon any pretext whatsoever and the Clubs must be a great boon to women who lead such narrow, prison-lives. Here they can come without fear of meeting the other sex, enjoy each other's society in pleasant, ample surroundings and talk over their troubles and, let us hope, forget them by so doing. One there was, who complained bitterly that her husband was so cruel to her, she could hardly bring herself to worship his feet in the mornings.

It seems that after the first few months of marriage, husband and wife occupy separate rooms. The wife rises first and after her toilet, her worship and her household duties are finished, she goes to wake her lord. Standing at some distance from his bed, she makes her obeisance and rouses him with a salutation. She then bathes the big toe of his right foot and marks it with sandalwood, "offering incense and lights before him, as if he were a god." [1]

The great Hindu Lawgiver, Manu, has said, "As far only as a wife honours her lord, so far is she exalted to heaven."

Loyalists at heart, when *Mother India* was under

[1] *The Rites of the Twice-Born.*

discussion at one of these Indian Ladies' Clubs, though not one of the Indian members present had read it, they denounced it unanimously as a "bad book." Why? "Because their husbands had said so." Hindu men have bitterly resented the exposure which "made known to the world the suffering of Indian women."[1] In all essentials it is quite true.

Undoubtedly the book did much good, if only by shocking the English public out of its apathetic indifference to, and giving them some dim comprehension of Indian life in its crudest aspects. It did some harm as well, inasmuch as the Indians retaliated by dragging into the limelight the evils of the West, which is "as yet trying and experimenting and has not succeeded in solving its pressing social problems."[2] This also is lamentably true.

At all events, Indian Ladies' Clubs have solved the problem of recreation for the Indian woman who is veiled. She can play tennis, badminton, ping-pong, bridge, chess and other games. One Muhammedan member improved on the occasion by telling me that the Great Moghul Emperors played chess with living pieces, and if one happened to be a beautiful girl, the interest of the "Game of Kings" was duly intensified.

On this especial afternoon, there was a great gathering of Hindu, Muslim and Parsee ladies in enchanting *saris*, gracefully draped and filling the room with beautiful colour. Some were gorgeous, fringed with gold and bugles; others of pastel shades and the loveliest of all was pale silver grey silk, bordered with pearls, worn by the President.

Some English children had learned for our benefit the story of the Princess and the Swineherd, that had been cleverly adapted as a play and delighted the audience; eliciting peals of laughter when the boorish peasant lad dragged his unwilling wife off to the kitchen to cook his supper.

Then came a lull in the proceedings and a recent

[1] Sir Francis Younghusband. [2] Maharajah Bahadur of Darbhanga.

acquaintance, whom I had met at my last Indian tea-party, greeted me and made an appeal for a charity. She was a charming little lady, with the circular red mark on her forehead that denotes unwidowed happiness, and I responded gladly; but when she thrust a printed leaflet into my hand and I realized she was asking a contribution for a Gandhi collection, my face must have betrayed my feelings. She said at once—"You don't approve!" and then, with quick courtesy, " then, never mind. Of course I am myself a Brahmin, but I feel that for the poor I ought to give some help."

CHAPTER II

AN EXTRAORDINARY POPULAR DELUSION

Haidar was born to create an empire, Tippu to lose one.

MYSORE SAYING.

The sword is his who can use it and dominion for him who conquers.

Koran.

A strange bird is hatched sometimes in a nest in an unaccountable way.

JOSEPH CONRAD.

To subscribe to Gandhi's campaign! This request from a high-caste Hindu lady gave me a shock of surprise, and the news too, that he should be coming here as a guest of Mysore State, to carry off all the money and jewellery he can extract from Bangalore. I remember the City, years ago, as an immense rabbit-warren of dark-skinned humanity, surrounded by a hedge.

It lies to the south-west of Cantonment and was founded and named, says legend, towards the close of the twelfth century, by Vira Ballala, a Hoysala king, who had become separated from his attendants whilst hunting. He wandered about till nightfall seeking food and shelter, and at last came upon a hut, where was an old woman, who gave him a supper of *bengalu* (green beans in water) which he shared with his horse.

Nowadays the hedge has given place to a wall and the City, much brushed up, is almost unrecognizable. It has extended beyond the four ancient watch towers—one at each point of the compass—which, according to prophecy, should be its uttermost limits.

More reliable records tell us that, in 1687, Bangalore was acquired by purchase from Venkoji of Tanjore, for the sum of three *lakhs* of rupees (about £30,000) by the *Zemindar* of Mysore, Chic Deo Raj Wadeyar. He ruled by favour and protection of Kassim Khan, highly placed at the court of Aurungzebe, and was tributary to that great Moghul Emperor, to whom he sent splendid gifts, that he might assume the title of Sovereign of the World and sit on an ivory throne, with some measure of safety.

Chic Deo Raj died in 1704 and in less than sixty years, the Muslims, under Haidar Ali and Tippu his son, had swept over the land, proselytizing and slaying the Hindus until they had supreme domination, which they held by use of whip and sword till 1791, when Bangalore was captured by the British, under Lord Cornwallis. From 1799, with the extinction of Muslim rule, peace and prosperity were established and have continued to the present time.

Haidar Ali had been succeeded in 1782 by his son, Tippu Sultaun, for whom he had a deep affection, though he knew him to be cruel and depraved, and had even himself predicted that he would lose the Empire, so hardly won, by his insensate folly. At birth, he had called him for a famous devotee, Tippu Sultaun, a Sufi, who had the right to assume the royal title by virtue of having conquered all passions, thus becoming a spiritual lord.

No greater contrast to the holy man could well have been found than in his namesake, Tippu, who had inherited temporal sovereignty and gloried in being known as "The Tiger"; adopted the ferocious beast as his badge and had, for support to his throne, one larger than life with golden eyes and teeth of precious gems. Above this barbaric splendour hovered a mythical bird, a mass of jewels, for it was fabled that the head, which it overshadowed, must inevitably be circled by a crown.

Tippu used tiger stripes in the ornamentation of his Bangalore Palace, the "Abode of Happiness and Envy of Heaven," that took eleven years to construct within the ancient fort, originally of mud, which his father had enlarged and rebuilt of stone.

The public and private apartments were on the upper storey, overlooking a large, open court, where fountains played. The favourite wife had a room with a balcony, where she could give audience to the Muslim ladies and the concubines. She often entertained them by tormenting the young British officer[1] (afterwards Sir David Baird), who was released from a dungeon near to the Delhi Gate, that he should draw water from a well within sight of the ladies and they could taunt him with their gibes and laughter.

The Palace, though gaily decorated in gold and colour, was of poor material that is crumbling to dust, and it has been abandoned after serving the purpose of Public Offices for some years. The Fort is now included within the City and was given by the British, in 1888, to the Mysore civil authorities in exchange for the Residency and grounds that were then added to the Civil and Military Station.

Whatever may have been the misdeeds and cruelties of Muslim rulers, they had a pretty fancy for laying out a pleasaunce, and Haidar Ali's beautiful *Lal Bagh*, enlarged by Tippu, is no exception to the rule.

> Sweet is this Garden, through envy of it the Tulip is spotted,
> The Rose of the Sun and the Moon form its beautiful lamps.[2]

The word "Zoo" in connection with the *Lal Bagh* is now, happily, a misnomer and there are no miserable caged beasts and birds in the garden to detract from its beauty and charm. Years ago a huge gorilla was imprisoned in an iron cage, so cruelly small and inadequate, that at last public opinion and sympathy was aroused by its suffering. I asked permission to examine its paws and I found, in the palm stretched out to me from between iron bars, the line of life ; the line of fate, till the age of capture; and a third line across the hand from the ball of the thumb and ending in a star, which denoted drunkenness.

The planter, who had caught the gorilla, when young, wrote a letter to *The Madras Mail* expressing his regret that he had been obliged to send his pet to the *Lal Bagh*, because he could not prevent it from climbing the

[1] 1794. [2] Moghul Garden motto.

trees in the compound and getting hopelessly drunk on palm toddy.

The authorities excused themselves for the rigorous confinement, to which the poor beast was subjected, by explaining that they had, at first, put it into a large circular hut, but it spent all its time taking it to pieces brick by brick, in its efforts to escape.

The monkey is a sacred animal to the Hindus, and their monkey-god, Hanuman, is worshipped especially on his birthday, a night of full moon at the end of March. It is said that, at his birth, he saw the newly-risen sun and mistaking it for a ripe, red fruit, leapt upward to seize it. He found himself mistaken, but he prevented an eclipse by striking down the demon, Rahu, who was about to swallow the great Day-maker and bring darkness over the earth.

A Hindu, having worshipped the picture of Hanuman in his house in the evening, should rise before dawn of next day, bathe and worship at the monkey-god's shrine.

The story of Hanuman's birth as a monkey appears in the Ramayana, an epic poem of ancient India. The father of Rama (a reincarnation of the god Vishnu, and also King of Oude) performed a special sacrifice to secure a son and heir to his dominions. He had three wives, for whom Agni, the god of fire, gave him three balls of rice, one for each spouse. The second queen was a careless creature and dropped her sacred pellet on the ground, whereupon a kite seized it and carried it off to Anjana, whose husband was a monkey and Hanuman was born.

It is the bull that is specially sacred in Bangalore, the charger of Siva, worshipped with, or without the god. In the far-away past the sun god triumphed under the symbol of the bull, the second sign of the Zodiac, to which its sanctity may be traced in some degree. As its blood gives birth to the goddess of generation, it is looked upon as an emblem of fertility.

The Bull Temple is situated at the edge of a large tank on a stretch of waste, undulating ground, where blocks of stone are piled up on crests of elevations; or they have rolled over to form a mass apart and give to the scene an uncanny suggestion of upheaval at some remote period.

The building has no architectural pretensions and closely resembles the stall where an ox would ordinarily be stabled, but it must be at least twenty feet high and the black bull that entirely fills it and stares with great, unblinking eyes from behind the iron bars, is colossal, its huge neck wreathed with garlands.

Painted close together and minutely, on the outside wall are the sun and moon, the two eyes of the Great Person. "The two eyes are like the pole of the Great Wain, which turns the whole of creation: they cause the poles of light and darkness to rotate. They are the highest manifestations of fructifying force and in their conjunction are emblems of blessedness. . . . The Light of Heaven cannot be seen. It is contained in the two eyes." [1]

The courtyard and surroundings of the temple were deserted, dirty and looked forlorn and neglected. It occurred to me that if some of Gandhi's Harijans, "my people" as he has called them, were allowed to sweep and clean up the buildings and precincts, it would be of benefit to caste worshippers. But no! the elect of Brahma would consider that pollution and the result would be a more thorough cleansing than the temple has experienced in the memory of man.

Of this, I have no doubt since visiting Conjeeveram, one of the seven sacred cities of India, notable since the sixth century for its temples. The one that now stands out most conspicuously for all beholders, was subjected to experiment by one of Gandhi's agents, a Congress *wallah*. Through his influence in the town, it was thrown open to the Untouchables, who, however, were so reluctant to avail themselves of the honour, that it was necessary to bribe them with a feast; and then, temple entry, of which we hear so much, actually took

[1] The Secret of the Golden Flower.

place. The chief priest was furious. The building was purified within and without and fills one's vision, to the exclusion of all else around and about it; a huge monument of *chunam* plaster; a whited sepulchre of the Gandhi campaign.

It is the belief of the vast majority of Hindus, that God resides in the temple and that the idols are the live bodies of the Supreme Being. "They are washed, clothed and anointed daily and are considered to have the physical and mental needs of a man: they may even fall sick and die on some particular day."

This belief involves the exclusion of the Harijans and is a fundamental law. "If this be violated," said Mr. S. Muthiah Mundaluyar, a former minister of the Madras Government, "God will leave the idol and vacate the temple."

Gandhi has expressed himself strongly on this very point. "It is a belief for fools and not for educated men that God dwells in temples": on another occasion he has said: "I am a breaker of idols." . . . "I consider a scavenger better than a Brahmin." Yet again, in a changed mood, "I do not disbelieve in idol-worship," a phrase that may have been better suited to his hearers at that particular place and time.

A strange bird, truly, to be hatched out of a Hindu nest. He is of the *baniya* caste himself, "immigrant traders and moneylenders from Northern India who have settled down in the southern *bazars*, where they carry on a lucrative business." By profession he is a lawyer and a very astute one at that, but the Government of India "persisted in looking upon him as a very holy and sincere man, who has always meant well," even though they were obliged now and again to put him into prison. His Civil Disobedience campaign cost them "in one year . . . over a million pounds" without taking into account the dislocation of trade throughout the country.[1]

In Gandhi's own words "Caste is . . . inherent in human nature, and Hinduism has simply reduced it to

[1] *The Indian Empire Review*, December, 1934.

a science." Certainly in the Hindu system, religious and social, caste is not considered an accident of birth, but the result of the transmigration of the soul, its *kharma*. It is because a man has grievously offended in a former existence that he is born a scavenger in this one: it is his punishment: it is the judgment of God. "Let no man think lightly of sin, saying in his heart, 'It cannot overtake me.' "

So it is with a woman. No one feels any compunction in heaping hardships on a widow. She has sinned in some former existence and must work out her *kharma* and "bear every reproach as God-given." The privilege of the virtuous is not to relieve pain, but to despise the sufferers.

> As a man sows so shall he reap.
> He who plants mangoes, mangoes shall he eat;
> Whoso plants thorns, thorns shall wound his feet.[1]

In *Young India* Gandhi has written : "In my opinion the idea, that inter-dining and inter-marrying are necessary for national growth, is a superstition borrowed from the West." Yet he broke his caste by feeding with Untouchables and for that penalties are demanded, which must be paid. These are the feeding of Brahmins, and to quaff a bowl of purifying drink, made from the five products of the sacred cow, of which the urine and excreta are the principal components.

Posing as a saint and reformer, Gandhi has achieved an amazing success by the science of unconscious, mental processes; the appeal to the mass mind, less intelligent than that of individuals and prone to an emotional hysteria that is contagious. There have been many previous instances in the world's history, and some fifty years ago they were collected and written down under the title of *Extraordinary Popular Delusions*. Another chapter might now be added to this work by an expert in psychology. There is no doubt that Gandhi has cleverly studied the suppressed desires of different

[1] *The Rites of the Twice-Born.*

sections of the community, not only Hindu, but also British, and they have responded in their numbers to hypnotic suggestion.

To the women of India he said, "I agree with you. There is no salvation for men without women's salvation. I assure you, I miss no opportunity of driving the truth home to men."

An immediate response to this came from Mrs. S. Muthulukshmi Reddi of the Legislative Council, Madras, who has at heart the women's forward movement.

"He has come to our help at the right moment and has championed the women's cause bravely and wisely. Is it any wonder that the women throughout India have answered his call for service at this moment?"

They have indeed answered his call with the self-sacrifice that is inherent in the women of India. They have assisted to swell the huge collections of money that he is accumulating. Many of them have stripped themselves of their jewels, the only property to which they have a legal claim and can fall back upon in the hour of dire necessity.

Friend of the poorest of the poor, he would solve the problem of unemployment. Everyone shall be clothed in homespun.

Khaddar, say the experts in finance, is an uneconomic proposition; it means dearer clothes for everybody, if the wearers are to earn a living wage.

Nevertheless, the masses heard and adored Gandhi for his boycott of British goods and unemployed, suffering Manchester cheered him to the echo. The irony of it!

He appealed to Christians and especially to those with a missionary spirit, who actually credited him with a desire to adopt their creed.

Placarded with religion in capital letters and with the label of *Mahatma*, "Holy One," "Great Soul," he pleads that scavengers may be admitted to Hindu temples and high-caste wells in company with Brahmins. Quite powerless in the matter really, as temples are under a

Religious Endowment Act and priestly control, he "but blathers of the impossible to humbug Western humanitarians." [1]

Who have been royally humbugged! Even had Gandhi "not had behind him the best publicity board in the world," such an appeal would be enthusiastically received by the frothy sentimentalists and religious cranks, whose ideas run away with them and who are only too readily fooled.

He is indeed an illustration "of the principle of labels . . . and of the system of propaganda through group leaders. . . . We have but to put a label on a thing and see that it is set loose and our great, interesting and interested country will do the rest."

During Gandhi's visit to London in 1931, a non-conformist minister flung himself at this *Mahatma's* feet. "O Saint!" said he, "Teach me how to be a Saint," and in a London drawing-room I, myself, have heard him compared to Christ.

At that time a sympathetic Press spread broadcast the information that he was lodged at the East End London Settlement. He slept there, but his days were spent in a charming flat in St. James's.

On one "inauspicious day" of the Hindu calendar, Gandhi, somewhat unwisely, received a visitor from his own country, Miss Cornelia Sorabji, who wrote a most amusing account of her interview with him for an American journal.[2] Here was someone who had no use for labels and did not hesitate to say so frankly.

"I have studied you," she said to him, "as *Mahatma*, Politician, Economist. . . . The *Mahatma* need not detain us. As you are aware, I know a good deal about Orthodox Hindus and have met the genuine Hindu holy man. You are not *that*, are you? You are not a Saint, Mr. Gandhi, you and I are lawyers." . . .

"What did you mean, Mr. Gandhi, when you said the other

---

[1] Lieut.-Gen. Sir George McMunn, K.C.B., K.C.S.I., D.S.O.

[2] *The Atlantic Monthly*, April, 1932.

day that you wished and demanded ' a partnership' with England, and in the same breath that you wished and demanded complete independence?" . . .

"I meant control of the army, of finance, of foreign relations —of everything."

"The British, in fact, as your disciples put it, 'kicked out,' said I."

On this occasion Gandhi was not dealing with the ignorant mass mind, but with one highly trained, notably clever, and exceptionally well informed at all points. When Miss Cornelia Sorabji had finished with him, he must have felt himself turned inside out of his brown skin, like an old glove.

Undismayed by such pin-pricks, he carries on his subtle campaign of setting one section of the community against another and his great work of collecting funds from the hypnotized masses. He has netted Rs.27,868 during this brief visit to Mysore State and Rs.65,108 in the Andradesa district, besides jewellery valued at Rs.2,000 (over £7,400).[1]

To what end?

[1] *The Indian Review.*

CHAPTER III

VILLAGE LIFE

GANDHI. "I have an outcaste girl at my *Ashram.*"

CORNELIA SORABJI. "What is that? The missionaries take hundreds of thousands of outcastes under their protection, clothe and educate them and fit them to stand on their own feet. Besides you are an outcaste yourself now. What credit can be claimed by an outcaste for adopting an outcaste child?"

HORRIFIED DISCIPLE. " She calls you an outcaste!"

The men lay back
On benches, the children played. The
women in silk *saris,* with their long
Plaits unwound were dancing 'twixt
the shadow of the palms, the old, old
Kummie dance.

A Son of India—D. H. SOUTHGATE.

THE *Kummie* and the *Kolattam* were being danced by groups of swaying figures in the large, tree-shaded compound of the Indian Girls' School, as the car passed slowly along the winding drive to the verandah of the bungalow.

It was a joyous scene and I leaned out to watch it with an æsthetic pleasure, a new phase of Young India: the lissomness and graceful movements and the novelty of this form of physical drill, to the clacking of short sticks and the rhythm of a song.

I had come to Chingleput, thirty-five miles south-west of Madras, to learn something of life as it is lived by ninety per cent of the inhabitants of the Presidency, resident in about fifty-five thousand villages of South India.

For a stranger, this is only possible under the auspices of the medical and educational missionaries, who devote their lives to the betterment of the depressed classes,

MAYPOLE DANCE BY HINDU (NOT CHRISTIAN) GIRLS

Gandhi's Harijans, the Untouchables, Lepers of whatever caste, shunned as the Unclean. It is a daily hand-to-hand conflict that they carry on against dirt and disease, ignorance, superstition, magic and all sorts of strange fears that the Hindus are heir to; so deep rooted, that in times of stress these may rise to the surface, even after lying dormant for years.

Practically every village has its own deity, whose shrine is at the entrance: it may be a figure, or perhaps only a symbol. At the back of the Girls' School, where is a cluster of Indian huts, I found an upright stone, with a triangle rudely cut out upon it, the Seal of David.

So far as its inhabitants are concerned, every village is surrounded by evil spirits that people the earth and the air, lurking in trees and stones and behind rocks; malicious demons that will bring sickness on them and their cattle and they must be pacified.

The gods, also, are queer-tempered beings to be propitiated with offerings of broken coconuts and flowers and whatever else the worshipper can afford. Mariamma, goddess of smallpox, has, possibly, more shrines than any other and her wrath can only be appeased by blood sacrifices, that were human at one time. Taking off my shoes, I penetrated one day into a glorified stone dog kennel in Salem District and at the extreme end of it, there she was, about two and a half feet high, painted blood red—a horrid sight.

However, she now has a powerful rival in vaccination; and a woman doctor I happened to meet told me of an amusing experience she had, when an outbreak was threatening. The subdivisional magistrate (*tahsildar*) appealed to her to vaccinate the inhabitants of his village, to which she consented, on condition that he would pay for the lymph, and she duly carried out her work.

Subsequently she heard that, quite early in the proceedings, he had sent one of his men to tell the people he was in such anxiety for their welfare that he could not sleep; and though it would cost him three hundred rupees to save them from this pestilential disease, he would do so. He then definitely refused to pay the bill she sent him for about forty rupees for the lymph, as he had agreed to do; but he collected a sum of four annas per head from each one of her patients.

Having heard this story, I realize the truth of a statement in a book on South India, in which the writer says, "An entirely 'honest' magistrate in the space of four years should 'save' about twice the total sum, which he received as salary."

In Chingleput District I did not encounter another Mariamma, but at one village we visited there was a small temple with a life-size tiger in stone to guard the inhabitants. At another to which the doctor had an urgent call, and where she had not been previously, she came across a shrine to Hanuman, suddenly, in the jungle.

Her first round began at seven o'clock in the morning, and sometimes I went with her on her errands of mercy, across rough country tracks in her own little car, so well known, watched and waited for and hailed by children, young and old. For that they are, of whatever age in years, and as children must be treated. What else than a deplorably ignorant child is the mother, who brands her epileptic baby with hot needles round the wrists and neck to keep away the devils? Or the man, who has one eye treated at the hospital and the other by the village quack? If his patient should lose his sight, the stars can be blamed, who settle destiny. In any case the *Vythian* will impress on the relatives that it is necessary to perform some religious ceremony to appease the gods, and the blind man might still recover his sight.

Half blind, or wholly so, they are in their thousands, and this is attributed mainly to venereal disease. Their own principal remedies would make an oculist shudder, such as pepper, cardamoms, cantharides and chilis for external application to the eyes.

On the outskirts of the main village is a clump of much smaller thatched huts, each with a little backyard—— This is the *parcherry*, where live the outcastes; "servants of the landowners, who are paid in grain and work from early dawn to dark; plough, sow paddy, water, weed, sleep in the fields when crops are ripe, thrash corn. . . . They serve the same families for generations and dare not accept service elsewhere."[1]

No caste man, or woman, would deign to enter the *parcherry* on any pretence whatsoever: equally so, if the impossible did occur, the outcastes would resent the intrusion, attack and turn out their betters. "*Brahmin* and *Sudra* have ineradicable prejudices, which they nurse with extraordinary fondness and cherish with unyielding tenacity."[2]

There was one village, that we visited every Wednesday, with no Hindu god to propitiate and no *parcherry*, since all its inhabitants are Christians and consequently outcastes. It consisted of one long and very wide avenue, with high, feathery palm trees on either side and at the far end a big schoolroom, with Bible pictures on its walls. They are all poor labourers, field workers, who live here under the protection of the Scottish Mission.

As a bye-issue, they are encouraged to take up poultry-farming and they are beginning to understand, at long last, that if they feed their cocks and hens, look after them and keep the breed pure, the result will be larger, more saleable eggs.

When the car stopped, it was at once surrounded and egg after egg handed in, put into a balance and paid for according to its weight. In all dealings with these people I was constantly reminded of the Salvation Army Notice above the telephone: "Ye have need of patience."

At every welfare centre is a dispensary and a nurse trained by the Mission to render first aid in endless cases and decide if the doctor should be sent for and the patient taken away to the hospital.

Lace making is another industry carried on by some girls, who have learnt whilst at school, and who are glad to continue this work, as a means of adding to the family

[1] T. Ramakrishna, B.A. [2] *India, Its Life and Thought.*

exchequer, always lamentably small and nearly, if not quite, empty. There is a folk saying that "Few families are blessed with good fortune in the three matters of children, of money and of milk."

About sixty girls were employed at their lace pillows every day in the school, under teachers capable of designing patterns for special requirements and orders. The work was beautifully exact and very fine, but alas! the market at Home for this dainty fabric has been badly hit by the heavy duty recently imposed on such luxuries.

At another mission centre in the district, boys were learning useful trades, such as carpentering, and in the old Fort at Chingleput there is a Government Reformatory School for youthful offenders.

It happened that I arrived during Health Week and was able to attend an exhibition and entertainment "for ladies only," when Mrs. Veerasinghi Chinappa, M.B., B.Sc., Assistant Director of Public Health, spoke at some length on "Maternity and Child Welfare." It was impossible for anyone to hear what she said, as her audience evidently had no interest in it and made a terrific din. The tent was crowded with the women inhabitants of Chingleput town and a host of their small children, and their daughters from the five Government and Mission Schools. As all were dressed in their prettiest *saris*, they presented a gay spectacle, and the young girls had flowers in their hair. They have a particularly charming custom of massing together small, pale tinted, fragrant blooms, such as cluster roses, mimosa, or champac round the twisted coil, or at the top of their long black plaits.

> What of the tresses of a woman?
> They are as flowers in a garland and a glory.[1]

The girls danced the *Kolattam* marching song and the *Kummie* in competition, and the school whose team work was the best and who never deviated from the rhythm and the clack, clack of their short sticks, won the prize.

[1] Folk Song.

Not for them a sergeant-major's drill of stiff, sharp movements! These ancient dances were evolved out of the supple grace of lithe, young bodies that seem to have no bones.

In the figures and steps of the *Kolattam* are suggestions of our own country dances, and even more so in the *Kummie*, when are twisted and untwisted long strands of coloured cords, with a continuous, circular direction of the dancers, that conjures up the maypole festivities of Henry VIII and Anne Boleyn.

The girls (all Hindu) had put on "fancy dress" for the *Kummie*, as I learned after expressing my admiration of the many-hued *saris* blending rainbow-like in the dance. They had been draped like those of Muslim ladies, who draw them up over their heads, that their hair—fatal attraction to their menkind—shall be veiled.

There followed on a most amusing dramatic entertainment, illustrative of first aid in accidents, which had been learned in school, and how a child may be saved by artificial respiration after falling into a well, a common fatality in India. These girls seemed born actors, which was due perhaps to a very noticeable absence of self-consciousness. Quite naturally, they portrayed various incidents in the battle against insects, dirt and disease, which they are taught daily they should wage in their future homes.

Attired in a long, purple velvet coat, embroidered in silver thread and velvet trousers, the ankle of one leg resting on the knee of the other in prescribed historic pose, the enthroned Maharajah called peremptorily to his *Dewan*:

"Come hither, Prime Minister! Many of my people are falling ill: there is much sickness among them. Attend to it! That is my will."

Entered a sweetstuff seller, who established himself and his stall at the street corner with his wares, and the little ones gathered around with their *annas* and *pies*, ready to spend their all. Pheugh! what a cloud of flies sticking to the sugar! By order of the *Dewan*, a policeman arrived on the scene to drive the old man away with contumely, that the children shall not fall sick from eating his dirty *jilebis*.

A buzzing mosquito was the next enemy to health that made its appearance on the stage, to be scotched by a sanitary inspector deputed to save the Maharajah's people from malaria. He was followed by his assistant, as a sandwich man, holding up an enormous placard of a rat, carrier of bubonic plague.

This health propaganda was further enforced by a series of pictures dealing most realistically with the Hindu home and customs. First on the list, "A Perfect Day in the Life of a House Fly." His *chota* is taken in the family latrine. From there, impregnated with germs of cholera and dysentery, he betakes himself to the kitchen, where he buzzes around and settles on the various items of food in course of preparation.

Most tragic picture of all for the health and well-being of future generations was a wedding scene; such a travesty, that to my eyes it seemed as if it must be merely children at play, at dressing-up in imitation of their elders. The bride, attired for the ceremony, was eight years old, the bridegroom only twelve. "We shall both wear the yoke of life together." [1]

It is generally supposed that a way of escape from such a yoke as this had been provided by the Sarda Act, passed in 1929 for the reason, it was said, "that there exists a grave and corroding evil in the country, which is clamorous for a remedy." The Bill was drafted by Indian lawyers, but the British Government shouldered the blame and the odium it aroused in Indian communities. Child marriage to be wiped out by a few strokes of the pen! "When the Institutes, which Manu, the great sage, the Hindu Lawgiver who came before Buddha, had declared to be a direct emanation from the deity and remain to this day the foundation of Hindu jurisprudence!" How could that be possible?

During the six months after the "April Fools' Act"

[1] From the ritual of marriage.

was passed, and before it came into force, five million marriages were celebrated of children, all under age. Even had they taken place subsequently, "the penalties therefore were practically unimposable."

There is surely a most pressing need for propaganda. "It is laid down," in the Mahabharata, "as a law, that a man of thirty should marry a girl of ten; a man of twenty-one should marry a girl of seven and some say the proper age is eight." To this Manu has added yet another injunction; that "a father may give his girl before proper age if the bridegroom is good-looking and worthy." In the month of April of last year (1934)[1] "a marriage was celebrated between a fourteen-year-old girl and a seventy-year-old man."

Even if a father were sufficiently intelligent to realize the benefits that would accrue to his daughters and their offspring by adult marriage, the social framework of Caste holds them in its grip. He might have difficulty in marrying them at all, and a girl must be married to fulfil the religious duty of her parents.

Caste has punishments, other than the purifying drink: for those who break its laws there is also excommunication and an interdict against marriage. "This practically amounts to debarring the delinquent and his family from respectable marriages of any sort."

The Sarda Act has proved a lamentable failure; a tragic farce "that is now dead and buried fathoms deep" to the satisfaction of every Sanatanist Hindu. Some optimist introduced a Bill for the Protection of Minor Girls, as an alternative; but it met with the least possible support and will certainly not become law. The legislators decided that public opinion shall settle the matter in individual cases; which simply means that children, who are voiceless, shall look for succour to what is non-existent, in a country where there is no compassion for suffering. There is no god of pity in the Hindu Pantheon.

Orthodox belief dies hard when extreme importance

[1] *The Madras Mail,* April 24th, 1934.

is attached to religion, which is the foundation of everything Hindu. "Every other thing gives way to this important aspect of Hindu life. In religion the Hindu lives, moves and has his being." [1]

It is the custom of our people: that suffices.

[1] T. Ramakrishna.

A TYPICAL COUNTRY ROAD, SOUTH INDIA

CHAPTER IV

SALUTATION TO SIVA

Trust firmly in one God and thus be saved, O mind!
Do not be born again by trusting in false gods.
'Tis only Siva who can understand
The goodness in the sacred name of God.
E'en so, the virtuous and the good alone
Are able to discern the highest truths.

Siva is Everywhere—HINDU TEXT.

All things made he—Siva, the Preserver,
Mahadeo! Mahadeo! he made all,—
Thorn for the camel, fodder for the kine,
And mother's heart for sleepy head, O little son of mine.

RUDYARD KIPLING.

BEFORE I had been many days at Chingleput, I was taken one morning on a pilgrimage to the famous temple of Vedagiri Iswara. In actual distance, it was only nine miles away by road; much less as the crow flies, and I could see it high above the surrounding country, in fair weather. At festivals, the lamps presented by votaries shone out in the darkness, as if to outrival the stars. So I had often looked across the plain at the rock precipice and had been told the story of the sacred kites, that are fed there every morning on their arrival from Benares, where they have *chota*: afterwards they fly farther south for an evening meal at Rameswaram and wing their way back, whilst others sleep, to the most sacred city of all India.

Long, long ago, there were eight gods, who guarded the eight points of the compass. They did homage to the great god Siva, but one day, in a fit of ill temper, he cursed them all and turned them into kites. They were very penitent and begged for his forgiveness, but he directed that they should live at Vedagiri Iswara, and only visit Benares and Rameswaram.

It is for this reason there are pilgrims to the temple and many come from the far-away north. The priest, who ministers to the birds, must speak at least three languages, Tamil, Canarese and Hindustani, that he can murmur *mantras* in these tongues to the *rishis*, and beg offerings from strangers for their daily food. A pilgrim will gladly vow a gift of mutton for the kites, if some member of the family is sick, when he makes his salutation to the great god Siva, in expectation of a quick recovery.

For the last two hundred years only one pair of kites has carried on the tradition: and always it has been, and is, the same pair. Other birds of the species, nesting all about the crags and precincts of the temple, fly to and fro, onlookers of the strange ritual; but none approaches the sacred bowl of *pongal* and *ghi* that the officiating priest sets upon a large, humped prominence, just below the peak and the temple.

Usually the ceremony takes place between ten and eleven o'clock, but rain fell the night before our pilgrimage and the morning was dull and cloudy. On such days, the journey from Benares is more difficult; the birds are always longer on the wing.

The sky cleared as we were motoring across the plain. Later the Day-maker came forth in his glory and once again I waxed enthusiastic in my admiration of the long avenues of glorious trees that line the main roads in South India. Some are very old; are said to date back to the time of Akbar Khan. Whether banyan, or tamarind, or palm, they give an ever-welcome shelter to thousands of pilgrims and travellers, who perforce walk, or jog slowly along in bullock carts and *jutkas* as of yore. At long intervals along the roadside, there are seen two uprights and a heavy slab of stone, man-high, resting on them; there the weary carrier's burden can be shifted from his head awhile.

It is amusing and odd to come across whole families

of monkeys straying happily about, deaf to motor hoots, knowing themselves immune from harm. On the outskirts of the villages, they are part and parcel of the village life. So much so, that recently at Tirupathi, when an old monkey died, who had been a universal pet, he was given a grand funeral procession with beating of *tom-toms* and singing of hymns. Carried to the burning *ghat* in a gaily-decorated chair, he was cremated like any other member might be of the Hindu community.

We passed no other pilgrims on the road: they had taken less risk of the probable delay of the ritual than we had, yet there was not any sign of the birds when we reached Tirukalikunram, a large village of the plains, which lies close under the shadow of the temple rock.

The main road led to a large open space where many beggars surrounded us, holding out their little bowls for alms.

At the farther side were wide and very high granite steps leading to the peak, into which the temple had been veritably inserted. With much effort, I climbed a flight of five and turned a corner, where was a more extensive view of the precipice. "How many are there?" I asked breathlessly, and at the answer, "Four hundred and fifty," collapsed just where I stood. There was at once a helter-skelter of bare, brown legs and feet and presently four men arrived with the lower half of a large packing-case, swung with ropes to bamboo poles that had yokes. Thankfully I climbed in, curling myself round in it, and the bearers were so kind as to chant a ditty in my praise. I was indeed glad to hear the word "*Rani*" repeated many times, for there is a tale of a tourist, who graciously, fatuously smiled on his bearers, tipped them handsomely and learned later that every verse he had thought complimentary, had ended with a chorus of "Big fat pig."

The cheery bearers carried me up five hundred feet of rock and set me down beside a kind of altar on high pillars, where pilgrims had collected, and soon there was a wave of excitement for the sacred birds had arrived, had alighted on the top of the hill opposite. Now there were two officials; non-Brahmin priests wearing necklaces of thirty-two beads, nearly black, that are called the "eyes of Rudra." One placed a bowl of rice on a large humped rock and knelt before it in the attitude of worship: the other stood at some distance, motionless, upright as a pillar of carved stone.

Presently, a whirring of wings and one kite skimmed gracefully above our heads, then swooped down. But no, it rose again without touching the proffered bowl and with a gesture, as of entreaty, the priest flung himself along the rock, muttering *mantras*. Why? What did this mean?

Other birds circled over us, flying restlessly from one hill to another, but with no idea of taking the food so temptingly exposed. Time passed. The sacred birds came no nearer than the opposite peak and still the priest, with hands folded according to his ritual, lay prostrate, praying.

At last, slowly, cautiously, one of the pair alighted, approached the bowl, picked out its little ball of rice and rising, swiftly disappeared. A pause and then its mate, that had not before left a lofty perch across the deep ravine, flew down also and was fed.

They had come singly, with hesitation, protesting, *because there were sinners present*, Christians, outcastes. On such occasions the sacred kites are never seen together at their morning meal.

The priest came down amongst us, bowl in hand, and climbed on to the altar. Round it pilgrims gathered, whom he fed with the sacred fragments that were left, excepting the Brahmins. They could not touch the rice, boiled by a non-Brahmin, priest though he be. For them, it was polluted by his touch. Instead, they were given grains of soft, white sugar, for it is essential on a pilgrimage that sweetmeats are obtainable, "without misgivings as to the ceremonial cleanliness of the people from whom they are bought." Who was to know how, and by whom, this foreign product was prepared? No eye present had witnessed it: not the chief priest, shaven, half-naked, barring the temple entrance with his awe-inspiring person till the strange ceremony was at an end.

He stood there watching, at the head of a long flight of steps, twenty feet above us all, whilst from a terrace outlined with unlighted lamps, we looked far over the plain to the temple tops of the Seven Pagodas, ancient Dravidian, rock-cut sanctuaries, built twelve centuries ago, at Mahabalipuram.

At our feet, close under the precipice where we were standing, lay the village of Tirukalikunram. It is a model of its kind, from the Hindu acceptance of such a term, and most satisfactorily planned, that the inmates of each and every house may see from its little compound, the temple of Vedagiri Iswara, as well as five high towers of the cult and shrines of Siva and his wife Parvati.

This goddess, who eventually became Siva's bride, had vowed to marry him from her earliest childhood. When her father told her, that by the advice of a great sage, she was destined for Vishnu, she ran away into the forest with her maid. There she occupied herself in making three *lingas* of sand, which she worshipped, and all night long she sang praises to the god. Siva was so flattered, that he appeared to her and promised to grant any request that she would make. She had but the one desire, that he would marry her, and this he agreed to do before he again vanished from her sight. Her father had been hunting for her all night and was so rejoiced to find her and that she had escaped harm, that he could not but give his consent to the union. Then Parvati married *Mahadeo*, the white god with reddish hair, who has five faces and sometimes as many as five pairs of hands.

He is the Self-Born, who carries a trident and should be worshipped with leaves of the *bel* tree, that is like to the shamrock, and with tears. His throat is blue from a poison, which the other gods feared to drink, for it meant death to them, to mankind and the universe, but the great god offered himself for the salvation of the whole world. He drank of the cup and survived: only his throat was deeply stained. In another legend the blue mark is accounted for differently. The gods quarrelled and Vishnu was so enraged with Siva that he seized him by the throat. Brahma was looking on, and nearly fell off his chair, shocked by such unseemly conduct.

"As the moon shines above mountains, he bears on his forehead the new moon;" the 'third eye of Siva,' set vertically. It was a love gift of the goddess Ammavaru, who danced before him, and he promised to grant her desire, if she would give him three things. He asked for a rug, some *betel* leaves and another eye; but when he opened it he reduced the giver to ashes. This involved the destruction of all womankind and he quickly repented his rash deed. He collected the cinders together and from them were incarnated three lovely women, who became the wives of Brahma, Vishnu and himself.

That is why Brahmins of the Siva sect smear three wide, white horizontal bars across their foreheads and daub ashes on their chests. A sight seen often, for *Mahadeo* is the favourite god of the large majority of Hindus. He is an ascetic and asks little of his worshippers; a few flowers, an oblation of water suffices for his needs. Sivaism is cheap. Practically every large village of South India has a Siva temple, usually the gift of a wealthy grain merchant of the *baniya* caste.

At the entrance to the village may be found, also, a large, raised platform beneath the shade of sacred evergreen *neem* or *margosa* trees, where are images of the many-headed cobra and upstanding, oblong stones with rudely carved snakes entwined. *Mahadeo* is associated with the worship of serpents and is decked and girdled with them, for they are emblematic of eternity. Outside his temple, facing the entrance and a few feet from it, is the *Nandi*, or stone bull; his "vehicle" as it is called.

All the principal gods have some means of leaving the temple precincts, when they wish to go abroad amongst their votaries. At Tirukalikunram, Siva has his immense, wooden car and also an ark, in which he can sail upon the waters of the sacred tank; seven times round at festivals.

Looking down upon it at high noon, the sun seemed to concentrate about it, dyed deep green by a prolific weed; and on the open, high-roofed shrine set in its very midst.

It is there that the *linga* is taken from the temple when there is a water festival in honour of the moon. For it is said, in legend, that the silver disc represents Siva's field-marshal, Virabhadra, rising from the great god's matted hair at sunset to defeat Kali, goddess of night, who would love to plunge the world in darkness and despair.

Of a truth, "to many, astronomy provides something of the vision without which people perish" [1] and such folk-tales as this originated in a desire to memorize a record of astronomical phenomena, that are so startling to ignorant minds.

The Aryans had worshipped the moon and stars before their immigration, and it was the moon's path through the lunar mansions that they primarily studied, till the Indian Sun, fiercely insistent, demanded a transfer of men's interest and adoration to his flaming self, as the Supreme Spirit.

"The blessed Sun spoke: 'I will give thee the science upon which Time is founded, the grand system of the planets.' " [2]

Associated with Siva in Vedic times, the moon became identified also with *soma*, the most important plant of the Rigveda, worshipped for its intoxicating qualities. By command of Vishnu it was flung into a sea of milk and churned with other medicinal herbs for the making of the Elixir of Life, to be known for ever more as the "moon plant." The mountain, Mandura, was used as a stick, the serpent, Varuki, as a churning rope and the magic drink was intended for the gods, and their sove-

[1] Jeans. [2] *Surya-Siddhânta.*

reign Indra, that, mighty and immortal, they should overcome the demons with whom they were at war.

The *amrita* was ready and the gods stood in rows to quaff it, passing on the cup one to another, when it was seized by a demon, who had slipped in amongst them, disguised as one of themselves. It was at his lips, but the sun and moon discovered the fraud and turned their piercing rays full upon the intruder. Vishnu, furious, cut off the demon's head at one stroke with a discus, and sent it spinning through the air, whilst the trunk fell to earth and the whole world trembled with the shock. The head became Rahu, a monster, the ascending node in the planetary system: the tail, Ketu, the descending node, another demon. They hate the sun and moon with a bitter hatred for their betrayal and are for ever trying to wreak vengeance on their enemies by swallowing them up in an eclipse. As they only succeed partially and the victim of the moment, whether sun or moon, must be disgorged, the eternal chase begins again and again and is ever foredoomed to failure.

An eclipse of the moon was due on the night of the 30th January and Rahu was now in hot pursuit of his foe, who was nearly at the full and in the plenitude of her beauty. As the late afternoon was drawing in to its close, hundreds of men, women and children could be seen on the roads converging towards the temple tank. The large open space at the entrance to the village was filled with poor little booths for the sale of various kinds of offerings to the gods; sacred leaves and incense, camphor to burn at the shrines; coconuts to break before the phallic symbol for hope of issue; flowers to adorn it. There were sweetstuff sellers, baskets full of glass bangles, children's toys and fairings.

The *linga* had been removed from the temple and now rested on the roofed-in altar in the middle of the tank. The priests, in charge, could be seen combing out their long jet black tresses after the bath of purification in the sacred, green water. Fronting them the sky had assumed a pale silver luminance, and behind the shrine there was a glory in the heaven of red and gold. Now it was dying, they lighted their torches and their flares and stood—waiting.

The ark had been lifted laboriously down the long flight of steps that surrounded the tank on all four sides, as a stone barrier between the water and high banks. They were packed with a dense mass of humanity, a

> "Hot damp crowd;
> The beggar with his begging-bowl, the
> cripple with his twisted withered frame,
> The leper and the blind."

A sudden radiance flared up in the west, illuminating the red, green, blue and orange *saris* of the women. It was an unearthly light, altering, transforming shapes and colours; the sun's farewell to the multitude and to the dying day as he gave place to the "Nightmaker," and the disc of the glowing moon floated solitary in the sky.

Presently the ark was launched successfully and came sailing by, close to the steps; and stopped every now and again that the people might pass their gifts on to the raft to be received by the officiating priest. Near him stood a wealthy Hindu merchant, who had paid all the expenses of the festival and for the thousands of tiny lamps that lined tank and temple and roof tops, shedding a warm, soft radiance of many twinkling stars. Musicians squatted on the deck and weird strains of a flute and the beat of *tom-toms* filled the quiet air. Two *devadaṣis*, temple dancing girls, leaned against the framework of the towering, unwieldy edifice above their heads; a high-peaked coronal, covered with red embroidered cloths. One woman had her child beside her, destined to follow her own profession, since "the mother of a servant of the gods is favoured by the gods."

The ark continued to float along gently, till it reached that central shrine, where was Siva, and only one offering of many hundreds was refused. A poor woman near by where I was sitting, broke a coconut and sent it by a local priest, but the high-caste Brahmin of superb form and appearance on the raft would have none of it.

I turned to a mild-faced holy man, a *Sadhu*, with a sacred volume in his hand, hoping that he might comfort her, who asked the gods for the gift of a child, with "that anxiety of reproduction, which characterizes the life of this land." He paid no heed, for at this moment all men's thoughts were diverted to the moon, who began to lose her brilliance.

Instead of making its seven prescribed journeys, the ark, bearing the *linga*, concealed in silk, gold ornaments and flowers, could make but one only. It was imperative that the god should be housed within the temple before the actual eclipse took place. Rahu, the monster, was gaining fast on the fugitive moon: she was entering into shadow, she was in great danger. Who could tell but that to-night the demon might win and swallow up the silvery dusk for ever? The multitude grew ever more anxious and excited. Only a great noise could help her to defeat her dread enemy.

Beat the tom-toms! Beat the tom-toms! Beat the tom-toms! *Beat the tom-toms!*

Pandemonium reigned throughout the night.

CHAPTER V

SPRINGTIME AND STORIES IN STONE

Let us meditate on the glory of the vivifier. May he enlighten our understanding.

Invocation to Surya, the Sun-God.

Looking with one eye is always bad.

Proverb.

L'architecture a été la grande écriture du genre humaine. . . . Toute pensée humaine a sa page dans ce livre immense et son monument.

VICTOR HUGO.

SPRING came to Chingleput during my visit and to all the other Tamil Villages of the Plains in the Madras Presidency. It was nearly mid-January; the blessed sun entered the sign of Capricornus, represented by a dolphin in the Hindu Zodiac, and the vernal equinox was marked as usual by bathing, feasting and jollity. Winter's last dark, inauspicious month was over and the pious man repaired to the courtyard of his house for prayer, that the beneficent rays of Surya might fall on him and he obtain special merit by his worship.

The womenfolk had been busy for at least a couple of days for Pongal, the rice-boiling festival. Old clothes had been burnt; whitewashing and spring-cleaning had upset the households; old pots and pans carried in procession to the nearest waste ground and ditches to be solemnly thrown away. At least one new vessel had been bought by every home for the fresh, pounded corn with milk to be set on the fire. Was the boiling quick, or slow? On that depends the luck of the New Year. Each family watched their pot anxiously. "The milk is boiling," shouts somebody, and a visitor arriving on the scene with good wishes for all, asks "Has the milk boiled?" "It has boiled," is the triumphant reply.

On all three days of Pongal, the salutation of the threshold, the *Kolam*, is an important feature, drawn with rice flour in the form of a building, a chariot, or a diagram of the deity, and also ornamented with little balls of cow-dung at regular intervals and a citron blossom fixed in each one. With these the women seek to propitiate the god who removes obstacles (Vighneswara), and they hang ears of the newly harvested corn at their doorways as a disinfectant against illness.

On the first day of Pongal, the Tamil New Year's Day, the cows and bullocks are supposed to have a holiday, and if this does not always happen, they are given at least a sumptuous meal of rice and fruit. They are washed, too, smeared with sandalwood paste and vermilion, garlanded, and their horns are painted in bright colours, or gilded, so for many days to come they are very gay and picturesque.

The cow is nearly as important as the deity himself. She, also, is a giver of great gifts, and is thought to bring peace and contentment to any Hindu home. " Cow protection is an article of faith in Hinduism. Apart from its religious sanctity, it is an ennobling creed," says Mr. Gandhi in *Young India*, and again: "It is the dearest possession of the Hindu heart, it is the one common belief to all Hindus."

I came across an interesting account of such South Indian beliefs and customs written by a fervent Christian, annotated by an equally fervent Hindu. The author gave as a reason for the extreme sanctity of the cow, that it is the incarnation immediately prior to that of a human being. I have not seen, or heard, this theory confirmed elsewhere, and strangely (as it seemed to me) his Brahmin commentator had ignored this passage; though on other pages he had not hesitated to express his feelings, if mildly to begin with, more violently towards the end of the book. It was natural enough that he considered *there was no necessity* for christianizing all South India, as the author piously hoped.

It happens just now that the Roman Catholic community of South India is seriously perturbed lest some two hundred thousand of their flock revert to Hinduism, and a situation has arisen which is described as intolerable. This is, to all appearance, due to caste, which is bred in the bone of every Hindu. Its evolution has proceeded along Hindu lines and now rears its head under the pseudonym of class distinctions. As a matter of fact, churches are known to be set apart for low-caste worshippers, where none other would attend the mass, and how far Rome, which has in the past assimilated pagan symbolism, may meet present difficulties, remains to be seen. Rumour has said that occasionally a form of worship is arranged for, which meets the requirements of converts; but men only may attend; the service is conducted under circumstances of strict privacy and may serve the purpose of cementing superficial adherence, that wavers for a very definite reason not stated.

The Indian world is well aware that, sooner or later, Federation will be the established order, with Hinduism in the saddle and Brahmins holding the reins. Though many converts, known as rice Christians, have benefited materially in the past by the adoption of an alien creed, this is not probable in the future. They were poor, of low origin, moreover, and not of much account in the general community; *pariahs* in fact. Now, in better circumstances, it is likely that social pressure will be brought to bear upon them, to which they will succumb. Any caste man who becomes a Christian from conviction, is ostracized by all his relatives and friends. In some cases funeral rites are held in his name, as if he had died and *shradha* were his due.

It must be taken into consideration that "the Hindu mind, like the Hindu faith, has a fatal facility for accepting, semi-assimilating and finally absorbing, all of religious belief and conviction that may come into contact with it. And this never necessarily involves the abandoning of the old beliefs." It can be noted again and again in the blend of Dravidian, or aboriginal, folklore and Hindu ceremonial: of Buddhistic forms in the huge cars used at festivals and in architecture; survivals of the heresy successfully combated by the Brahmins of India.

This is obvious at Mahabalipuram, called generally "The Seven Pagodas," about twenty miles distant from Chingleput, where even the plan of the Shore Temple, so attractive from its site almost within reach of the waves, has been altered out of its original design and significance by the activities of religious dissentients. But it is still a beautiful picture of the skill and genius of the Kurumbers, the aboriginal inhabitants, enhanced by the natural artistry of surf breaking over its great granite blocks.

Eventually Sivaites and Vishnavaites used the Shore Temple in common; one sect worshipping the black marble *lingam*; the other, Vishnu recumbent on his many-headed snake.

There is no more fascinating story-book in the world than this islet formed by canal, backwater and ocean. Its very atmosphere is steeped in Hindu fable and fancy, illustrated in carved stone by Indian artizans of the remote past; who pictured here not only the Romance of the Mahabharata, but also "petrifactions of the last forms of Buddhist architecture and the first forms of that of the Dravidian."

A flourishing seaport this must have been on the Coromandel Coast, until the waves overwhelmed and drowned it fathoms deep; for at low tide, those that have eyes to see, report gleaming spires and the tops of buildings of a great, ancient city that temporarily emerge out of the shallow water. Even before that time, there was a mythological era, when the wicked King Bali, Ruler of all the earth, held his court at Mahabalipuram and was so powerful that the gods hesitated to cope with him by force, so needs must have recourse to Brahmin stratagem.

Vishnu became incarnate in his fifth aspect and, appearing to the mighty king, whom all the world feared and hated, he begged for a piece of land, but only so

THE SHORE TEMPLE, MAHABALIPURAM

much as he might be able to cover in three strides. Bali laughed scornfully and granted so trifling a request from a dwarf, but Vishnu suddenly assumed the proportions of a giant, with eight arms, holding a sword, a quoit, a shield, a bow and a lotus flower. One huge foot covered the whole earth; the second step he took obliterated the heavens, and when the King, alarmed, humbly offered his head to the god, he found himself pushed deep down into hell. It is but symbolic, this Eastern story, of the rising, culmination and setting of the Sun.

The sculptured scene may be found between the canal and the sea on a low granite ridge, with other quaint carvings, and amongst them one, unfinished, of Vishnu with the head of a boar uplifting the earth goddess, whilst his right leg prisons Golden Eye, a giant, who had carried her into an abyss, where he was ultimately slain and our dear earth saved for us by the great Protector.

But it is as Krishna that he makes his greatest appeal to the Hindu mind: in his eighth incarnation the god is so essentially human that Mr. Gandhi says he, himself, regards Sri Krishna not "as an *avatar* but as an ordinary man." On the east side of the ridge, he amused himself by making a slide and near by is a flight of steps, where he played at "mounting the throne." The favourite legend of his pranks with milkmaids is depicted in a cave temple and his great fear of uplifting a mountain to shelter, with this improvised umbrella, his cowherd friends from Indra's wrath, when the angry rain god would have swamped them in a storm. *Swami*, or man, he lives in the heart of every Hindu man, woman and child who enters this pillared cave at the south-east corner of the hill.

These records are full of life and movement, but the greater interest centres in the story of the five Pandava brothers, the celebrated heroes of the Mahabharata and Draupadi the wife they shared in common, who was married to each one in turn, beginning with the eldest.

Her fate had been ordained in a previous incarnation by the god Siva, when she prayed five times to him for a husband. Siva, always original and playful, decided that five husbands she should have and all at once, when she was reborn as the Princess Draupadi, daughter of Raja Druped of Panchala. The Raja had been conquered by the Pandavas and a tournament was arranged to display the skill with bow and arrow of many assembled warriors, with the Princess as prize for the winner. Many tried to shoot the eye of a golden fish through a whirling disk at the top of a pole and all were unsuccessful.

Then Arjuna stepped into the arena, one of the Pandavas, disguised as a charioteer, only to be greeted by a cry from Draupadi: "No, no, I cannot wed with one who is base born," for Krishna alone was aware of the high origin of the five brothers.

"Unless a Brahmin knew his own strength and skill he would not make the essay," retorted Arjuna, sending his arrow direct into the eye of the fish. "So shall a Brahmin do this great thing, which all the mighty Rajas have failed to do." The host of Brahmins, chanting Vedic hymns, cheered him to the echo, for there was ever jealousy between the two highest castes: those springing from the mouth of the god and the Kshatriyas, the soldiers, out of Brahma's arms and body.

Then Draupadi, beautifully robed and jewelled, radiant with happiness, embraced and garlanded her hero, and the sage Vyasa gave it, as his opinion, that the five Pandavas were really five incarnations of Indra and therefore only one man.

It is this story that the Kurumbers of old chose to commemorate by buildings "to be understood by every soul, intelligence and imagination: symbolic, but as readily comprehended as nature . . . in popular language which is the truest art." [1] They are rock-cut monuments called *raths*, monolithic, quite individual in design and the one farthest to the north has a conical roof like a thatched cottage. It is Draupadi's. There

[1] Victor Hugo.

are some who think that they were carved for the sake of ornament rather than use, as they are modelled on *rathas*, the huge cars that the Hindus drag at festivals, and every one is different from the rest, with the upper parts sculptured and the lower blocked out to preserve the fiction that it is a vehicle.

The second *rath* is Arjuna's, reminiscent of a Buddhist monastery as is also the fourth named after Yudhishthir, another brother, which has four storeys. Round windows ornament three of these and it gave me quite an eerie feeling to see the face of a monk gazing out of every one: faces that had been there since the seventh century watching generation after generation of devotees and sightseers that had come to visit the *raths*. The fifth monolith recalls the architecture of a Buddhist chapel: the sixth and largest is only partly excavated, and so many of the monuments are unfinished that it is supposed the busy workers may have been suddenly disturbed and driven away for ever from the scene of their labours by a cataclysm; war, or perhaps earthquake, as the third *rath* is rent from top to bottom.

The later history and the Penance of Arjuna, who turned his face towards the jungle for twelve years of exile as an ascetic, is pictured about half a mile away, sculptured on the eastern face of the ridge. It is a marvellous bas-relief that forcibly reminded me of Noah's entry into the Ark, for human beings and animals are all depicted in pairs and at one time a cascade rushed down the cleft at the side of the rock in a deluge of water.

Arjuna stands in penitential attitude with upraised arms, his ribs protruding, his whole form emaciated with his long fast. All the world and his wife have come in couples to watch him. Round and about are gods and demi-gods, *rajas* with their *ranis*, sages, ascetics; in all, eighty male and female figures, besides birds, deer, lions, tigers, cheetahs, monkeys, hares and life-like elephants with their young sheltering under their huge bodies. "The mysterious characteristics of the stones, which naturally resemble the skin of the royal animals in texture and colour, have been utilized with the strangest art."

The Raja Mahabali is there amongst the crowd; and the snake deity with his daughter and Gautama Buddha accompanied by five disciples. Lastly, near Arjuna is Draupadi's thieving cat, also doing penance for her sins with outstretched paws.

It only needed this to convince me that the five Pandavas and their wife must have lived, moved and had their being in the island even for a little while. Here are the five pots they used for their burnt offerings; Draupadi's bath and her vat for turmeric in the middle of the ridge. Climb a few steps to the fireplace where brother Bhima cooked for them all and examine the butter-ball, half-eaten by that bad puss who chipped it with her sharp teeth, whilst Draupadi was busy with her churn.

Mahabalipuram is peopled with the ghosts of the Hindu mythology, and though the *raths*, *mantapams*, monoliths and temples have been taken over by the British Government as a national monument, and there are no Brahmins or priests for *puja* on the island, Hindu devotees still go there to worship gods and heroes on the nights of the new moon.

Soon the low caste *Sudras* will celebrate the *Holi*, South India's Saturnalia, when the demoness Holika must be propitiated by bonfires and driven away from the babes she would have devoured, by blowing of horns and beating of drums, so that quiet folk and all respectable women keep within the shelter of their homes.

For fifteen days, too, before the full moon of March, Krishna is honoured and his image set swinging, for the wheel will have turned and the sun be well away on his course northward, the air hot with the passionate kisses of the great god Surya. The Season of Spring is then at its height: it is the triumph of Love.

CHAPTER VI

THE INCENSE ROCK

All the talk we have heard
Uttered by bat or beast or bird—
Hide or fin or scale or feather,
Jabber it quickly and altogether!
Excellent! Wonderful! Once again!
Now we are talking just like men.
  Let's pretend we are . . . never mind
  Brother thy tail hangs down behind!
  This is the way of the monkey kind.

RUDYARD KIPLING.

Wash daily from nose to tail-tip; drink deeply but never too deep;
And remember the night is for hunting, and forget not the day is for sleep.

The Law of the Jungle, RUDYARD KIPLING.

THE weather was getting unpleasantly hot, for now that Spring—close herald of the Indian Summer—had come to stay in the Plains, one quickly realized that "the sun-wheel begins to run." I had come back to Bangalore and cool nights on the plateau. Not to remain for long; only on my way to the Biligirrirangan Hills, via Mysore, where I arrived at dinner-time, after a journey of four hours.

On the next morning and one of brilliant sunshine, my luggage roped securely on the carrier, I started for the coffee plantation, where I had been invited to stay, with an added inducement of "always cool weather just now."

We were speeding away on the road as the clock struck nine and it was little that I could see of Mysore City as we passed quickly through the outskirts. It was only possible to catch fleeting impressions of beautiful, tropical growth and of many Hindu temples set in the midst of trees. The going was easy, on a level road for many a mile and not much variety in the open country, till we came to Nanjungud, a large village with a great temple, surrounded by lofty stone walls, that celebrates a car festival when the god drives out in state at the end of this month. Evidently the cult is very much alive here for in the street we met a procession following a tawdry, wooden reliquary, a quasi-shrine, that was carried towards us on men's shoulders and decked out with coloured cloth and flowers.

A few miles more and we reached Chamarajnagar, where the railway ends, and at a junction of roads took that of Panjur, which leads to Attikan and Garstead, in the Biligirrirangan Hills, whither I was bound.

Many years ago, the pioneer who opened up this country for coffee and who was a great *shikari*, was gored by a bison in a lonely stretch of jungle just off the road. His escape from death was miraculous and a small monument with a bull couchant marks the spot on a bank a few feet above the roadway. This is now an object of worship by the hill people of the district; garlands of flowers are hung about its neck and to its deaf ears they pray that they too may be saved from the jungle beasts.

We climbed the *ghat* for a couple of hours, where cardamons were planted alongside coffee thickets under the beneficent shade of the wonderful evergreen trees. The season's crop had just been gathered in: the unripe green and the polished red cherries which hold the coffee bean, wrapped within a parchment sheath, had all vanished; even gleaning was at an end.

At the bungalow, facing a deep ravine and with a sheltering hill rising up behind it, surrounded by flowering creepers, by shrubs, magnolia and margosa white blossomed temple trees, I could only regret the shortness of my visit: a stepping-stone of these hills to one two miles higher, where the road ends and from whence I must be carried, higher still.

It had just been discovered, when finishing off the sweep of the road for the car to turn, that a magic stone, an important proof and exhibit of a Sholaga legend, had

SHOLAGAS IN FESTAL ARRAY

been crushed out of existence. In mythological times it had been the brass bowl of a priest who ministered to the god Madhappa. The god died and his faithful servitor was so terrified that he flung away his sieve in one direction and his bowl in another. Both immediately were turned to stone, and there, fortunately, the sieve can still be seen. As for the man himself, he rushed in his panic to another village thirty miles away and rooted to earth became his own monument, an object of veneration to the present day.

After expressing wonder at the transformed sieve, I could more truly do so at the magnificent view of deep ravines and forest-clad hillsides, soon to be shut away by jungle, through which a path led to my journey's end, a shooting-lodge in the blue, where the canopy above, so near sometimes, was that most exquisite colour.

Waiting here was a little group of carriers for luggage, for baskets of food and for me, who seated myself in an upright canvas contrivance attached to two poles, that rested fore and aft on the men's shoulders and a swing-board for my feet. They brought me the rest of the way, about two miles at a trot: small, lean, but sturdy Sholagas, who live in these hills in huts of jungle wood, bamboo and thatch. Their physique has declined of late years owing to constant intermarriage amongst themselves. There are two septs; the Eid-Kulas (from the Hill jungle) and the Yerl-Kulas (from the Plains jungle). Though the Eids claim to be of a higher caste than the Yerls, this is not taken into consideration when seeking a bride and they are, probably, all very near akin.

The fusion of blood shows itself in an unforeseen way, for the lower caste, oddly enough, have more Aryan traits than the Eid-Kulas. It is always supposed that caste originated in the desire of the conquering race (and subsequently the superior classes) to keep themselves pure and apart from the original Dravidians, who were dark skinned. The word "caste" has come into use through the Portuguese, and its equivalent in Sanskrit is "colour" [bar].

E

The Yerl-Kulas are of a sallow fairness, with straight hair tied at the back and brown eyes, but though some of the Eid-Kulas have a similar complexion, others have dark, round faces, squat noses and a crop of wavy, frizzly hair tied at the back of African heads. Both septs speak a dialect of Canarese. If called upon, these people work for the Forest Department, but they also are glad of employment for eight or nine months of the year on the coffee estates, which have been the means of opening up and developing the country. Then they return to their own villages to work on the land.

Of such was my escort, clad in loincloth, or shorts, and a jacket: their leader with a bright green turban hiding his crisp hair. He and another lad had smeared their faces with white clay, as devotees of Rameswaram, sacred city of South India on the sea; and in imitation of *Lingayats*, who acknowledge only one god, Siva, and reject the other two persons of the Hindu Trinity.

The latter part of the march was fascinating, as we moved more slowly along the narrow path cut through the jungle: a tangled mass of undergrowth around, branches that had fallen off, weirdly shaped and covered with lichen; stones behind which some snake might be lurking. Masses of trees bent towards and intermingled with each other, closely interlaced as a safe roofing of green mansions to shelter jungle fowl, wild pigeons, the "ice bird" with its maddening tuk, tuk, tuk at dusk, the "whistling schoolboy."

Across our route, bars of sunlight shone out and disappeared again, as the blue sky was over us, or shut away by an arch of greenery above our heads. The air was cool and fragrant with five types of incense: some sort of excrescences from rock and stone (known only to the Sholagas), and three other kinds taken from trees, such as the strobilanthes, that only flowers once in seven years, whose seeds can be heard to drop, drop, drop in the stillness. We had arrived then at the outskirts—on the forest-fringed boundary—of the hill that is crowned by a Sholaga shrine, sacred, scented Dupabarri, the Incense Rock.

Another few paces and we were in a wide clearing on the edge bordering a steep ravine with hills beyond it, ridge after ridge to the skyline. Dupabarri to the right and a mountain immediately behind, gorgeously clad and densely in green and russet and brown of thousands of forest trees in a mass. To the left a contrast, a high, bare, bleak rock with a stony ridge, where a stag sambhur, head and horns uplifted "had wheeled and was standing at bay" on the alert, searching the landscape for a possible foe.

There is a road up there and remains of a fortress erected at some period before there could be any record, and the building of it has escaped men's memories. All about the vicinity of the lodge are traces of a bygone cultivation by tillers of the soil, who must assuredly have dwelt upon it. Who were they then? "Not us," say the Sholagas, "but some pygmy men, who rode on hares and dwelt in the little houses you have dug up out of the earth."

True, houses have been excavated in recent years, made for the dead, not for the living: tombs with pottery jars, which had food in them for that last, long journey into the Unknown.

In the graves of their own dead, the Eid-Kulas place some personal belonging of the deceased, such as a knife, or an axe. On the twelfth day after death, a party of twelve will go off together into the jungle to seek for a headstone, which will be pointed out to them by their god.

There was, lately, a death on the estate of a Sholaga from the plains, and it is understood by the survivors that within two years at least, a number of them must make a pilgrimage, carrying some earth from the grave to their chief temple, of Biligirri Rangaswamy, east of Yelandur, on the brink of a precipice. It is of great antiquity and from it the hills take their name.

In his monumental work on the *Castes and Tribes of Southern India* Mr. Edgar Thurston gives, at some length, the tradition that is current amongst the Sholagas themselves, of their origin. Briefly as possible, the story is as follows:

Once upon a time there were two brothers, Karayan and Madheswara, who were captured by a demon, called Savanan. He made a shepherd of the elder brother, but the younger one he clapped into prison for disrespect and ordered him to make a pair of shoes. To do this, Madheswara begged to be released for a few days, and as soon as he was free he asked for help from the god Krishnamurti, which was graciously accorded. Together they made a lovely pair of slippers, but, by the god's advice, they were of wax.

Savanan was so delighted that he put on his new shoes at once, not realizing that a trap had been laid for him. Madheswara had piled up a bonfire on the rock till it was red-hot; the wax melted and Savanan fell, clutching at his enemy's throat in an effort to strangle him. However, the gods had all been summoned to see the fun and Krishnamurti begged them to pile stones on the demon's head, till he released Madheswara and had been himself crushed to powder.

Meanwhile Karayan had been tending his flocks and he chanced to hear of the demon's death. He was very angry with his brother for not consulting with him first, and Madheswara had to fly before his wrath. Again Krishnamurti came to his rescue and he leapt ten miles to the "Bending Hill" which gave under his weight, and again five miles to the "Subsiding Hill" and it subsided; Karayan pursuing him, knife in hand. He fled once more and hid under a rock, which was slashed at so violently that the marks are still there for anyone to see, and at last he scrambled into a rat hole. Then Karayan sent for a lot of shepherds and bade them pen their cattle and sheep over the top. This was too much for the fugitive and even his god could not help him in such a stench, so the two brothers came to terms. Karayan stipulated that he should have prior claim to all worship and votive offerings from their devotees, and it is so to the present day.

The story of the mysterious fortress on the hilltop was told to us one evening in the dusk by Ketta, the *shikari*, who accompanies the owner of this lodge on all his expeditions after tiger. Ketta is of the older generation of Sholagas, who remember these tales, in which the young folk have no interest whatever.

It was a great god, Sumadaru, who in the days before creation built this ancient road and fortress. He was a terrible despot, and gave orders to his wife to grow wheat that could be sown and eaten in one day. As she was unable to work this miracle, she was "finished with" and he replaced her by another one.

At last the tribe could bear with him no longer and they begged for assistance from Madhappa, the god of the opposite hill, and he was cunning and laid a trap for the enemy. He had a rock greased all over and sent a pretty girl to stand on it.

"There's a dainty morsel for me," quoth Sumadaru, and straightway he began to climb towards her; but he slipped and his knee made a huge hole in the rock as he fell, such a giant of a god was he! And as he lay prone Madhappa slew him, but he said he did not want to look over at Sumadaru's hill again and he took himself off to Rameswaram, where he lives now in the Temple of that "City of the Gods."

The gigantic hole in Dupabarri is quite visible from the verandah, though nearing the end of the great mass of jungle and then grey rock jutting out and less clothed with greenery, where honey is in all its crevices. This spreads itself far beyond the compound and dividing barriers, then descends to the bottom of the steep ravine, which bounds the level stretch of ground on which the lodge is placed.

My servant came to me late one afternoon to announce a visitor at Dupabarri and I hastily took up field-glasses to aid my eyes in the failing light. Crouched up on the ledge of Sumadaru's hole was a monkey, a big, black fellow, about five feet high. We gazed at each other across space, but I made no overtures for a closer acquaintance, though he was to be seen at the same spot several evenings in succession and I began to think he was a resident, my nearest neighbour.

When he ceased to return I missed him sadly, but soon after his disappearance there arrived a family of bears. I had an urgent message not to take my usual morning walk in the jungle to an attractive rustic bridge over a stream, that picked its way with soft, chill murmurs over some favoured pebbles, leaving others unwashed and thirstily dry. A bear was engaged in digging a pit between the road and water bed, with so much noise of grunting that it was supposed at first she must have lost her cub. It turned out, however, that this was not anguish but swear words when roots, or other obstacles hindered her task. However, the very next afternoon my path was cleared again, for the family, led by Papa Bruin, made their way through the undergrowth to a bare, brown patch on Dupabarri, where they had a great game, chasing each other round a prominence. At last they vanished behind its jagged ledges and to my great regret they never returned.

This was due to a pack of wild dogs. Five scouts of a company of twenty came to the lodge tank and scared the servant, who was turning on the water, by getting into position on either side of him, so that he fled back to the kitchen, shouting for help. For nearly a week these hungry beasts kept away all game from Dupabarri.

It seemed strange that Ketta, bribed by a promise of ***baksheesh***, did not return to tell me more stories of the Sholagas and the gods, especially as he has been asked to do so by his master, who hath much honour in this hill country as a great *shikari*. He is so well known for his powers all over India, that applications come to him, even from the far-away North, for tiger fat to cure rheumatism and make people strong as the beast himself. The *Ayurvedic* physicians, whose system is based on hygiene and diet, the "science of life," prescribe the flesh in cases of asthma, tuberculosis and general debility. It is even salted, dried and preserved for some months for the use of their patients. On the West Coast the tongue—believed to be poisonous—must first be cut out and burned.

All the tiger heads at Garstead have been denuded of their whiskers by the servants. One bristle alone is a most valuable means of protection from an enemy: better still, might even be powerful enough, to bring about his downfall.

Even more efficacious, perhaps, in the affairs of life is a *mantra* such as the one which I am so fortunate as to possess. It is about an inch and a half square; contains, presumably, some mystic words on paper; is bound with coarse threads that completely conceal this and thickly powdered with saffron to keep the threads close together. Hidden somewhere in my enemy's room, preferably under the threshold where he frequently passes to and fro, this will influence him to concede my secret wishes: he will be as wax between my fingers and always completely in my power to deal with as I will.

No bristles came my way, for during my stay at Dupabarri, only one tiger visited the lodge and at night, when the servants declared they saw "starch-blue" eyes glaring at them in the dark. He escaped the shoot that was arranged in his honour and a panther fell instead to the two guns.

After the wild dogs were well away from the neighbourhood, a herd of wild pigs busied themselves on Sumadaru's hill, nosing for white lily bulbs, a toothsome delicacy, till the roadway looked like a ploughed furrow. Deep down in the ravine, where is a pool, the sambhurs came in the dusk to drink. It is then and in the early mornings that the birds call and answer from one jungle to another, across the clearing, and there are curious sounds of wild creatures, the ough-ough of monkeys and sometimes a cross, excited chattering.

At noontide silence falls. All this little world of birds and beasts is asleep. The hot sunshine illumines the vast plain stretching out below with an elephant jungle immediately under this elevation. In the middle distance is some cultivated land and a village; far away, a little white chapel where a French priest worships in the manner of the Catholic West.

Behind all and facing the lodge, rise the Burghur Hills, that extend along the horizon for background, as far as eye can see: section by section, in three or four undulating lines, the last and highest bounding our vision and meeting the sky. Great black patches there are on hill and dale: shadows cast by the fleecy white and grey clouds that float across, having detached themselves from the blue heaven and are free.

There were days when the Incense Rock moved, by some magic, nearer to the lodge, so that all its jagged formations, huge crevices and sparse, infertile growths were the more easily seen. The wealth of forest trees bordering the rock that have England's autumnal tints, reminding me of October days at Home, looked as if on a canvas of Berlin woolwork, and the wonderful red cinnamon leaves lost their oily polish in an atmosphere that enveloped the Burghurs in mist. Rain came and sleet: a heavy storm that ushered in spring to the hill country and the Sholagas prepared for *Ugudi*, their Spring festival, their New Year's Day.

They live on *ragi*, yams and jungle animals, provided that no European hand has touched the kill and defiled it. My host of the lodge shot that pest of the woods, a jungle cat, and his attendant retrieved and carried it off delightedly for the feast. It was not Ketta who was with him and it is said the *shikari* is sick with fever. This is the unhealthy season when, as a preventive measure, the coolies are being dosed daily with quinine. The doctor is away. Hindu private affairs are always of the utmost urgency and he has asked for a fortnight's leave to attend a domestic ceremony at Bangalore, which requires his presence: his patients must take their chance.

However, it is rumoured also that Ketta has been in consultation with his fellow Sholagas as to the unwisdom of telling me stories about the gods: he fears they are angry and he will be punished. As soon as Ugudi was over, this was confirmed, and we heard the awful news that during the festival, which lasted all night, Ketta was possessed by a devil. My fault? ! ! Oh, vengeful shades of Sumadaru and Madhappa, what am I to do about it?

When this happens to a man of the tribe, he rushes wildly away from all the rest, who follow him, beating *tom-toms* and making a terrible din. A nail is found to be driven into a tree and to this nail a lock of the victim's hair is attached and cut off—quickly. The god—or devil—then enters the tree. It is an infallible cure and to my relief Ketta has recovered from his madness, but even so, is not quite yet his old self again and I dare not ask for any more tales.

Fortunately his unpleasant experience did not prevent other Sholagas from giving us an entertainment the day before I left: a dance-drama of the Hills.

A party of them arrived about five o'clock: musicians with cymbals, *tom-toms* and a very primitive type of concertina, more like an expanding letter-case in shape, and the music, syncopated jazz.

Women never take part in such a dance, but two boys were dressed up in bright *saris*, one in green and blue, the other in red, bordered with purple, both pretending to be very shy and coy.

There was an introductory dance by a man, whose black face was lined with many yellow tiger stripes converging towards his nose, and there was nothing special about it, except a few wild leaps in the air. It was merely an opening measure for the chief dancer, who wore a curious high headdress rising in many points, a mask, breastplate and outstanding shoulder pieces all of a dull shade of gold, picked out with red, which had a decidedly barbaric effect. In his dancing, still to syncopated time, he suggested the action of riding at great speed and pulling up his horse on arrival at a village or house.

Meanwhile, the two girls had been standing aside, with

heads and faces closely veiled. Now they were brought forward singly, by the other male dancer, and in turn presented to the Chief. He had an interview with each. There ensued obvious love-making on his part and much pretended coyness from the maidens. One went so far as to simulate dislike. However, eventually both yielded to the great man's advances.

After this pantomimic dance some of the audience sent for their little sticks and gave us a man's exhibition of the *Kolattam*, but they were neither so expert nor so interesting as the Chingleput schoolgirls.

The Sholaga women had no intention of being overlooked. When dinner was over and the moon had risen they came up in a bunch from the coolie lines and danced the old, old *Kummie* dance, as had their ancestors in the days of Karayan and Madheswara.

CHAPTER VII

THE BLUE MOUNTAINS

The torn boughs trailing o'er the boughs aslant,
The saplings reeling in the path he trod,
Declare his might—our lord the elephant
Chief of the ways of God.

RUDYARD KIPLING.

I am the meat of sacrifice
The ransom of man's guilt,
For they give my life to the altar knife
Wherever a shrine is built.

RUDYARD KIPLING.

IT was with great regret that I bade farewell to Dupabarri and the wild creatures that had come within sight and sound of me, to return to the world of men and women and the many conventions that hedge us in. There is a fascination in a hermit's life and in the words of Walt Whitman:

I think I could turn and live with animals, they are so placid and self-contained.
I stand and look at them long and long.
They do not sweat and whine about their condition,
They do not lie awake in the dark and weep for their sins,
They do not make me sick discussing their duty to God,
Not one is dissatisfied, not one is demented with the mania of owning things.

As it happened, I had not entirely finished with jungle life, but was to encounter its tragic side on my journey out of solitude to the favourite Hill Stations of South India, Ootacamund, Coonoor and Kotagiri.

After the sacred cow, our lord the elephant takes second place in the estimation of most pious Hindus. They have not omitted him from their Pantheon and he is represented as half animal, half human; a pot-bellied jovial man with an elephant's head, born of Parvati, in the absence of Siva, her husband. She was having a bath and amused herself by picking small excrescences off her skin, which she fashioned into a baby and breathed life into the little form she had made. When Siva returned to find this infant of his wife, he was exceedingly displeased, especially as the child had refused him entrance. With the fury and ruthlessness which characterize the doings of this most unpleasant god, Siva decapitated the boy at once, without hesitation. Parvati wept bitterly and on hearing her story he relented, cut off an elephant's head and clapped it on the child's body.

Now the humorous, mischievous god Ganesh is patron saint of all schoolboys, students and the followers of Nationalism, who have adopted his symbol, the *Swastika*, for their very own. The actual meaning of the word is: "So be it: it is well," from *su* "well," and *asti*, "it is." Either the words "*Sri* Ganesh," or his symbol appear on the fly-leaf of day books, ledgers, and at the head of bankers' letters. His image is to be seen in all sorts of unexpected places as a good omen: it brings fortune to a shop and if a house door faces the side-walk (which is "inauspicious"), the elephant god removes the ill luck.

Since the Hitler régime was established in Germany, the sign of the cross with bent arms has become familiar to all the world. It is the hermetic cross of Freemasonry, emblematic of good fortune, but beware! if it be reversed, it becomes at once associated with black magic and devilry.

The *Swastika* is also a symbol of the winds; the four corners of the earth and of heaven, that are upheld—says the Hindu—by four elephants. Much that is mystic attaches to this strange figure, the "guarded cross" of Scandinavia, Central Europe, Egypt, Asia Minor, India, China and Thibet.

The massive royal beast "that hath between his eyes a serpent for a hand" and that few animals can pass without betraying fear, has been drawn into the magic circle of sacredness and mystery. The King of the Gods,

GANESH

Indra, has a white elephant: Lakshmi has two that pour water over her body.

Jungle men talk of our lord's strange ways, "Who sleeps so little and so lightly"; of dances that take place on huge, circular clearings, that the elephants make and tread down to a polished level surface for "ballrooms" in the dim recesses of the forests. Left to themselves, say the hunters, they never die, for who has ever seen a dead elephant? In the death agony does he perhaps drag himself to the impenetrable jungle, there to be buried by the herd in tangled undergrowth, or some deep pit? Who knows? Not the *shikaris.*

The day before I left Dupabarri, a strange exciting rumour was spread abroad, that circulated on hilltops, in jungles, valleys and plains, with the amazing rapidity of all whisperings in India. The impossible had happened! In giving birth, that simple, ordinary occurrence in wild animal life, a female elephant had died by the wayside of the jungle: near her lay the stillborn calf. The herd of some twenty or thirty elephants had been with her, but they had cleared off. When all had gone, with slow, ponderous, swaying steps, the mate was seen returning to mourn his dead. So it was thought by the *shikari* who witnessed the scene, but apparently the mate and all the herd refused to believe in so incredible a happening. Next day, they came again in the late afternoon, carrying in their trunks water from an adjacent stream, which they poured over the inert body in a futile effort to bring the dead elephant back to life again.

When I had passed, a few hours previously, the tragic scene was marked ahead for me, by a hideous black cloud of vultures that, startled by the oncoming car, rose high up into the air, wheeled about and swooped once more to their gruesome task of scavenging.

For this jungle edge lay on my line of route after a long and wonderful drive from the foot of the Attikan *ghat*, by which I had come to Dupabarri from Mysore City. The road branches off in a westerly direction, skirting Coimbatore District, and at first we were on level roads, passing a succession of little villages by the way. One was obviously Muhammedan, from the picturesque, whitewashed *Koubbas*, that were dotted about the environs. Others, that had Hindu inhabitants, were as evidently under the protection of Iyenar, a popular god in the Tamil country. He is the village watchman, who patrols when darkness falls upon the land and all the devils and malicious spirits are let loose to torment poor, superstitious folk like these. His votaries present clay horses, that stand outside his shrine at the entrance of many hamlets. We passed one magnificent charger by the roadside and other less showy steeds that visualize for the people their deity's mount, when he is safeguarding them and their property on his solitary, midnight rides.

Soon again we were ascending another great "landing stair," where a road has been engineered that is a miracle of twists and turns and has twenty-seven hairpin bends. It was exciting to rise higher and still higher; 2,000 feet, 3,000 feet, 4,000 feet and more, as indicated by stone posts recording the height, and to look down a sheer descent to the vast plain below; with ever-changing views as we rounded yet another corner.

Across space was a mountain range, bare, stony, precipitous and corrugated like iron roofing: in the depths were trees, clumps of houses, cultivation.

Gradually we began to descend, and as we neared the large village of Satyamangalam we met a long, far-reaching string of bullock-carts; hundreds of them all bound thither for a fair and festival in honour of Mariamma, goddess of small-pox.

Every cart was a replica of the one ahead and behind. The half-naked, upright, bronze figure of the driver squatting precariously on a narrow board and almost pushed on to the shaft by the mass of copper-coloured humanity squeezed together under the tilt of the waggon: legs, feet, hands, apparently detached pieces of anatomy hanging outside, for which there was no room within.

Many were walking and all were in their best, or most lately washed garments, and motor buses were packed full also, that plied to and from distant villages and the scene of propitiation, festivity and commerce. We caught but a brief glimpse of the fair; of many booths in course of erection; of a brisk trade in mats, baskets and quantities of red and gold bags, that serve the purpose of pochettes to hold various trifles, such as a few *annas*, a rosary, betel leaves wrapped round areca nuts, which all Indians chew as a digestive.

It is not a pleasant accomplishment for onlookers, but when seeing it I shall always be reminded of the beautiful grove of areca nut palms that lies at the foot of the Nilgiri *ghat*. This was more arresting of its kind than anything I had met with yet in Southern India: tropical luxuriance and warmth are so generously expressed and nature's lavish mood is sufficiently restrained by man for the purpose of commerce. Lofty crests of waving feathery plumes crown the slimness of tall grey-green trunks, high in the air, half expelling sunlight from a wealth of broad-leaved plantains and their yellow fruit.

The road from here onwards all the way to "Ooty," as the Station is called in popular parlance, was perfect.

There were several connecting bridges, over a gorge dry for the moment, for April showers are due, and the planters of tea and coffee are anxiously studying the clouds. It is many a year since the last bridge was built and then it was most unsatisfactory and collapsed after the *monsoon*. The root of the trouble was well known to the hill people, the builders; in fact, everybody. There had been no blood sacrifice to ensure its stability, and "human life is necessary to the preservation of an artificial lake, river embankment, or bridge."

After the third rebuilding, nothing went wrong and it was said—"Hush! hush! let us whisper it!"—there had been an old woman and she had disappeared about that time and now there were bones beneath the bridge and it has never broken down since. Of course not!

It is the self-same vision of the people that has given

the Hills their colour name of "Blue," [1] though at first I could see no reason for it. It could not be due to the rarely blossoming blue strobilanthes, nor to the blue lily that has been imported from Australia; nor to the magnificent, but infrequent jacarandas that are nearly purple. Rather, to my eyes, the rounded tops and steep slopes were verdant; splendidly green paling into greyness of the silver oak trees planted in groves that are parasols to shelter tea.

There came a day when the atmosphere was heavy with the scent of eucalyptus and the wind was stirring the leaves ever so slightly in sunshine of a purple sky, tempered in its brilliance by a dusty haze of particles shot gold and blue. Now I realize it must be some chemical component of the grey-blue granite rocks that produces this colour, as unique as the ancient race dwelling upon these hill-tops and proudly arrogating to themselves the title of "Lords of the Soil"—the Todas.

A curious and handsome people! Men with long, flowing wavy hair and patriarchal beards that might have stepped forth from some mid-Victorian Family Bible pictures of Abraham, Isaac and Jacob tending their flocks, as these aborigines tend their buffaloes. One of the lost tribes? No; fortunately for them their noses are Roman, rather than Hebrew; but they have at least one funeral ceremony in common with Mosaic practice. Possibly they are of Scythian origin and were immigrants, who succeeded cairn builders and lived for many centuries isolated 5,000–7,000 feet above sea-level and from the Hindus, who venerated the Hills themselves for their height and [till the British came] for their inaccessibility.

Despite research and suggestions, the origin of the Todas is still somewhat shrouded in mystery, though not so sacrosanct as the late Madame Blavatsky would have had us believe; an atmosphere partly engendered by their extreme reluctance to make known their customs. For them, it is a form of sacrilege to do so that will surely be punished by the gods, "who are invisible,"

[1] Nil = blue and giri = hill.

TODA HUT AND FAMILY, OOTACAMUND

TODAS

TODA FESTIVAL

they say, "but ever present with us." After Dr. Rivers [1] had completed his exhaustive inquiries and investigations into their habits and beliefs, members of the tribe were involved in unexpected misfortunes of every kind, which obliged them to have recourse to their diviners, their ever-present help in trouble. These mediums dance themselves into a state bordering on frenzy and in a semi-hypnotic condition give forth their inspired knowledge, it is said, in Malayalam. But that is not Toda talk, which is a tongue of itself (possibly Dravidian) and as well, they have a secret code for use amongst themselves in the presence of the other tribesmen, their subjects, who acknowledge this prehistoric suzerainty and pay tribute without question.

The Badagas, agricultural labourers, give offerings of grain as a return, it is supposed, for the use of the land they cultivate. In the secret code these little men are designated as "they who wear turbans." The Todas rarely cover their matted hair and are clothed in a fashion of their own, unlike all their neighbours. They are draped in a kind of mantle that crosses the back from the left side, passes under the right arm and the point is thrown over the left shoulder, rather like a toga.

Irulas are hunting men: so, also, is a Kurumba "the man who watches the way" and he is an expert in magic which can neither be circumvented nor remedied and is therefore, dreaded by the Todas, who know it to be superior to their own sorcery and medicines. Toda so-called secret cures, especially for rheumatism, have been in the limelight recently and it is probably the virtues of a plant, *Dodonæa Viscosa*, that have been rediscovered with all the sensational publicity of modern methods of advertisement. Its leaves are dotted above and below with small surface glands and the secretion that pours out when they are interwoven and pressed makes an excellent bandage, comforting and healing for rheumatic joints. It is one of the commonest of Indian plants and grows abundantly on the Nilgiris near Kotagiri and Pykara, so

[1] *The Todas*, W. H. Rivers.

that the Toda priests could not keep it a "dead secret" if they would. Moreover, it was known to Linnæus and named by him after a well-known botanist and physician.

There is yet a fifth tribe that is to be found on the Blue Mountains, "men beneath" as they are contemptuously termed by the Lords of the Soil in their private code. A poor thing indeed is a Kota and not even capable of "looking anxiously," the equivalent phrase for a glance of the evil eye. The Todas say they brought them up from the Plains to work as artizans and mechanics: to build and repair the strange dwellings that are as uncommon as themselves. A Toda hut is shaped like the tilt of a bullock waggon and is of bamboo fastened with rattan and thatched. The entrance is less than a yard high, but a tall man can stand upright inside, once he has wriggled himself into the interior.

As a reward for their services, the Kotas claim all cattle that die by accident or disease. Say the Todas: "When the buffaloes are alive they are ours, when dead they belong to the Kotas"—who eat them. But in *Amnôr*, the abode of bliss, they rejoin their owners that the milk supply may never fail.

"We and they are born of the earth" is the Todas' own belief of their origin and that of their buffaloes. After death, the souls of the deceased take a flying leap from an isolated peak 7,000 feet high, to a temporary heaven in the west, where the sun goes down. As it sinks behind Mount Mukarti they salaam to the "Great Man" as they call him. In the morning, when he rises, they greet him with a formula of prayer.

The sun is by no means their only god and of late they have begun to assimilate some of the Hindu cult and to frequent the temple at Nanjungud; sometimes returning with a shaven head, having sacrificed their locks as a thankoffering to the god for some benefit received, such as the birth of a child.

Their own temples, built rather like superior Toda dwellings with conical roofs, are dairies sacred to milk, which is their staff of life, and many of their buffaloes are included in a sacred herd. No woman dare set foot within one of the sanctuaries, nor follow in the immediate wake of the divine animals. When she fetches buttermilk for her household, she must stand to the right of a stone post facing the temple-dairy and at least twenty paces from the entrance. A Toda woman, though comely enough with her long, black ringlets, ranks lower with her lord than his cattle, and a bride prostrates herself before her newly-wedded husband, who places his foot upon her neck.

The little villages, with perhaps only half a dozen huts and a temple in each, that lie around Ootacamund, are beautifully situated and tucked securely away behind large groves of trees, that shelter and hide them from an alien world. Narrow valleys with streams, or swamps, divide up the undulating pastures of their peaceful country.

In one of these villages a temple was in course of erection: a unique event in a lifetime. When I paid my first visit, it was not yet a sanctuary and therefore possible to get a glimpse of the interior, which is partially screened off about the centre, that the most sacred vessels of the Toda ritual may be kept behind the partition. After consecration a near approach to it would be dangerous, as the malevolence of the deity would be provoked, with what dire results no one could foretell!

Thatching had not been started, but a festival to celebrate completion was announced to take place in a few days at latest. I gave myself an invitation to return, but whether the Todas did not want visitors to witness their rejoicings, or whether they were dilatory in finishing their work, the ceremony was postponed no less than five times and announced for the afternoon when it actually would be at an end. I had an inspiration to be at Taranadamund at ten o'clock in the morning, instead of at three, and was just in time to see the last layers of thatch in their corner and a number of silver charms being nailed to a wooden shield above the wide granite blocks, that form the façade of this curious building, which has cost a thousand rupees. Symbolic signs in white chalk were then drawn upon it and a buffalo's head and horns just above the absurd entrance, that is only two feet eight inches high.

From economic reasons, no doubt, the Todas have practised polyandry and girl babies, at one time, were quietly smothered out of existence at birth by some old woman.

The men of this generation have not inherited the strength of their forebears. Every village has its "lifted stone"; a large, round heavy ball used in their sports, which has acquired a semi-sacred character. On the occasion of my first visit to Taranadamund, a young Toda was called away from the building operations to give me an exhibition of his prowess. He raised the stone from his foot along his leg, rolled it up his thigh and the side of his body level with his breast—but no further. He could not lift it on to his shoulder.

Moreover, they have married only amongst themselves, so that the tribe has never been prolific and now is slowly dying out. All the men from the other villages had mustered in force for this important festival, yet there cannot have been present more than one hundred and fifty.

The women, at first, were busy preparing the feast, but as soon as the thatching was over, they were banished behind a primitive barrier of stumps and boughs at the back of the temple, where they could not get even a glimpse of the ritual dance.

This took place immediately in front of the building, which is on a lower ground level than the village, in a clearing just large enough to hold a circle of forty-two men. With fingers interlaced, they moved round slowly to the rhythm of their barbaric song and with many exclamations of "Hoh! Hoh!" hunched up the right shoulder with a jerk, as they took each swaying step.

Then came a pause. The circle broke up for a relay of newcomers, who chanted a litany whilst they danced.

TIGERS AT MUHURRUM

A white-headed kite soared high and then low above the unusual scene: an omen of good fortune, but that is a Hindu, not a Toda, superstition.

This was my last visit to the Lords of the Soil, for though the consecration of the temple had yet to take place on the following Sunday, it was a ceremony for Todas only. It takes place inside the building, where flints are struck in the good old prehistoric way to make a fire on which milk is boiled in the most sacred vessel of the dairy.

The return drive through Ootacamund was also one of farewell to that famous Hill Station, that is the seat of Government in April and May and the pleasure resort of the rank and fashion of South India in the hot weather. The climate is delightful and to many the place itself is reminiscent of Home; "another Hampshire," for are there not firs in plenty and blackberries and wild roses in the shady lanes? The splendid country seats of Rajas and the bungalows of British residents, scattered about the mountain sides, have wonderful gardens with a profusion of English flowers. Yet, no obliging stretch of imagination could make me think myself in England, with that curious blue haze about me and the eastern radiance of the sky.

Coonoor, 2,000 feet lower, is almost smothered in sub-tropical vegetation and has been built in a series of terraces with the *Bazar* filling up the valley and the Roman Catholic church of St. Anthony on the highest ridge. Between, in picturesque confusion, are hotels, bungalows, schools, Hindu temples and the twin spires of a mosque, for there are Muslims here who, at the close of this month of April, have been celebrating Muharrum with much *tom-toming* in their quarter of the town.

It is a yearly commemoration, enjoined by Islam, of the martyrdom of the Prophet's grandsons, Hasan and Hussain, at the battle of Karbala, and should be a period of mourning and kept as holy as the month of the Great Fast. On the last night but one, arrangements had been made for an exhibition of fire walking, such as had taken place at a Hindu temple at the end of March, at which His Highness the Yuveraj of Mysore had been present. This is, in itself, a species of martyrdom, only it happened that rain fell in torrents and effectually put a stop to the proceedings by extinguishing the fire.

No sounds of distress, or wailing, had reached my ears during the week; but I was considerably surprised on the last afternoon of Muharrum to find a carnival in full swing in the *Bazar*. There were sweet-stuff vendors and toys and fairings in the Market Square, and the Indian inhabitants, Hindus not excepted, were all enjoying the fun of dressing-up in outlandish clothes and the excitements of a merry-go-round. Wild looking tiger-men were engaged in mimic warfare before the premises of the chief Muslim baker, who enjoys a reputation for generosity. In a small enclosure, a series of duels with short swords, or sticks, delighted the crowd.

On all the ridges, that overlooked the main street of the little town, were gathered large groups of onlookers and that great magician, the sun, lit up the hillside and the bright-coloured draperies and turbans of those who awaited the procession, for clothes are always gay in the Tamil country. It was so much delayed, that he grew tired of shining and all radiance had faded out of the sky before a car made its appearance dragged along by pious Muslims. I was told that it carried the lucky hand of Fatima, mother of Hasan and Hussain, but have not been able to verify this information. There were no signs of mourning as it passed through a great throng of people to the mosque: the spectacle had been all joyous on a lovely summer day, and this, it seems, has become the general practice in South India. A shocking state of affairs indeed, which so horrified the Nizam of Hyderabad, that he "has been constrained to take up his pen on the subject, because as the ruler of the largest Muhammedan State in India he thinks it fit and proper to give advice to Muslims" in a firman just issued to his subjects.

"We Muslims," proceeds the firman, "claim to be followers of Islam and therefore it is incumbent on us to conform to the tenets of Islam. . . . We, who claim to follow in the footsteps of Hussain's grandfather, must not cease to observe the holy month of Muharrum with due reverence, especially in this State."

PART II

HINDU TEMPLES AND THEIR GODS

CHAPTER VIII

GREAT FESTIVALS

"They made a four-wheel image car, more than 30 cubits high. . . . The chief image stood in the middle of the car with two Bodhisattvas in attendance on it."

HUEN TSANG, A.D. 640.

"O Vishnu incarnate in the form of Buddha."

JAYADEVI, *Twelfth Century*.

"Beating my breast, aloud
How oft I called the crowd
To drag the village car; how oft I stray'd
In manhood's prime, to lave
Sunwards the flowing wave
And, circling Saiva's fanes, my homage paid."

Tamil, trans. R. C. CALDWELL.

"The rapacity of the temple priests is unbounded, whilst their culture is beneath contempt. They celebrate their festivals like children playing with dolls. They carry the gods in procession, or induce the gaping crowd to drag them along in huge idol cars."

TALBOYS WHEELER, *Hist. India, III*, 94.

FOR any European who has had the experience of spending the hot weather in the Plains of South India, there can be no difficulty in realizing why sun worship has been in existence since the Vedic period,[1] and that even the great Maya, to whom was proclaimed the Secret Doctrine, performed very severe religious austerities in propitiation of the sun. As spring quickly and insidiously becomes summer, his glory "whose fierceness increases every moment like a scorching brazier" becomes terrible in its intensity, corroding, disintegrating, till Hinduism and its votaries are brought to the verge of hysteria and the atmosphere is electric and charged with danger. Moreover, it is the season of epidemics, not-

[1] 1500 B.C.

ably of small-pox; that dreaded scourge which India, obsessed by the Devil of Fear and his obsequious attendants, Ignorance and Superstition, has materialized under one odious form or another, as a female deity. Any outbreak is due to the anger of the Goddess Mariamma, or Poleramma, or whatever she may be named in the particular town or village. She is calling for blood, say the people, and she must be propitiated. On her senseless head falls the blame of the blood-lust engendered by barbarous, unbalanced crowds at high tension, who demand an orgy of killing and torture to quiet frayed nerves: to restore the balance of reason and security.

It is holiday time. When the blazing sun has scorched the fields and the earth is hardened into dry brown clods, there are festivals, pilgrimages and fairs. As in other countries, they are closely associated with the religion of the people, which, it has been said, "is the outcome of their spiritual needs." Hinduism has prescribed for the psychological requirements of seventy per cent of its votaries, "for whom," say educated Indians, "anything spiritual has no meaning at all."

Crushing goats to death, gagged that their cries shall be stifled; spiking live animals and jolting them in carts till they die by slow degrees in excruciating agony; dragging the unborn lamb from its mother's womb, a horror dear to the Oriental heart: it is all part of the ritual. As such, it is enjoined by scholarly Hindus, educated themselves possibly out of belief in gods, but realizing the need of the illiterate masses for a creed and its formulas.

> "Destruction of life is inevitable in life. . . . For specific reasons a certain method of extinguishing the animal's life is undoubtedly prescribed and adhered to in these Vedic functions . . . Not being troubled by the inferiority complex, the Vaidics do not worry themselves over what . . . a neo-humanitarian in Madras says in condemnation of their ritual."

This is a Hindu expression of Vedic opinion.

The neo-humanitarians had been busying themselves with the greatest festival ever witnessed at Ellore. They

SRI VARADARAJASWAMI ON THE SACRED KITE

had gone so far in their endeavours to stop the slaughter of a thousand rams, fifteen hundred fowls and fourteen buffaloes, as to apply to the local magistrate for an injunction against a "public nuisance" and "obstruction" in the roadways of the town. He had refused it and they appealed to the High Court, which upheld his decision on the grounds that the Courts could not be used as a vehicle for propaganda.

The festival was an enormous success. Men, women and children came to it in their thousands, to propitiate the goddess Poleramma, who had afflicted her people with small-pox. The chief priest, his face besmeared and his clothes drenched with blood, invoked the goddess whilst he sprinkled cooked rice and blood along the streets. The season has been exceptionally dry and lately there has been a shortage of water in the unhappy town and in any case, there can be "no good effect on crops without the spilling of blood."[1] Now they may surely expect a bumper harvest at Ellore.

The priests, doubtless, have already made theirs, but with one exception. A servitor of Poleramma, who should have graced the procession, turned sulky and absented himself, for the reason that the temple trustees, either could not, or would not, pay his exorbitant fee. This has caused some anxiety to the inhabitants, lest the goddess be angry, but fortunately it seems that she did not miss him amongst the concourse by whom she was accompanied. Or else, soothed and flattered by the adulation of the crowds, that waved her picture in the heated air, she has condescended to overlook the matter, and so far as I know, has not again visited her wrath on their devoted heads.

The horrors of Ellore chanced to be coincident with the commemoration this year in other places, of the birth of the Lord Buddha, whose coming was announced by a star. "To-day Bodhisattva is born on earth, to give joy and peace to men and *devas*." The princely ascetic is generally accepted by Hindus as the ninth reincarna-

[1] W. W. Hunter, C.S.I., C.I.E., LL.D.

tion of Vishnu, the Benevolent, who reigns as the Supreme Being of the Vaishnava sect, at the golden city of Conjeeveram, the Benares of South India.

It was there that I wended my pilgrim way, being assured that at the shrine of Vishnu, the Preserver, there would be no animal sacrifice, though the torture of hook-swinging that may mutilate a man for life, is not unknown, but is now discountenanced by Government. But since my visit, I have learned that I had a fortunate escape from the blood-lust and that the ceremonies of next year will last nearly twenty days and include animal sacrifices for which a sum of fifteen thousand rupees is required and a fifth of that amount has been collected in the first few weeks. Yet I imagine this cannot be by desire of Vishnu, but must have originated in Siva Kanchi, where Siva's spouse, Kali, is calling for blood.

I arrived at the end of May just in time for the Grand Festival of the year, also called "Brahmin Kite" [1] after the god's favourite vehicle, which indicates the ethereal attribute of its rider, when he goes in procession through the town to visit his brother-in-law, Siva, and graciously permits the minor deities to pay their respects to him. He halts for some time at the lesser sanctuaries for *puja*; his progress signalled by *tom-toms* and the salute.

An outcast, I would not be welcome to reside within the precincts of the sacred towns, known to their inhabitants as "Siva's golden city" to the north and "Vishnu's golden city" to the south. Most fortunately, I dwelt in a charming oasis midway between the two, in the shade of gorgeous, flaming gold mohur trees in blossom and coconut palms. Yet I was within easy reach of both towns; within sight and hearing of the crowds, the processions and the persistent beat of the *tom-toms* that provided occupation, awe-struck interest, or exhausting physical labour for thousands.

As might be expected from its great age and sanctity, Conjeeveram is a city of temples and tanks, as sacred, where pilgrims drink of the holy, stagnant waters and

[1] Garuda Utsavam.

bathe in them that their bodies may become golden, their minds acquire knowledge and their souls attain salvation. There are seven, one for each day of the week.

When I took my walks abroad, away from the unhallowed road in which I lived, I seemed to come upon a shrine at every turning and only a few yards distant from the last. On my right hand, one adorned at its corners with the *Nandi* of Siva: across the way another, with images of Ganesh on either side its doors.

One morning I motored through the town northward, beyond the broad thoroughfare nearly two miles long called Raja Street, that has been the way of pilgrims and processions since the days of Huen Tsang, traveller and author. I had heard that there were sculptured figures of Kurumbers to be seen at a Siva temple on the outskirts of the town, where are paddy fields and I felt deeply interested in the artizans who were responsible for the *raths* at Mahabalipuram. Though I had previously visited this ancient temple, I had not then known about the indigenous Pallava race that had peopled the Coromandel coast in days of yore and the genius that depicted the stories in stone.

In fact, the temple had been disappointing: so forlorn and neglected in appearance that I doubted if it were used nowadays for worship of the gods: for that colossal game of make-believe, still enacted in the twentieth century by Brahmins, priests and people. "Let's pretend they are alive! they move and have their being, marry, beget children just like men." Quite recently, orthodox opinion has been divided as to the propriety of a suggestion at Kumbakonam that the chief idol, who is already married, should take another consort. The matter is to be threshed out and settled in the civil court. Doubtless it was a symbolism, but it has become to them —even the educated—a reality from which they do not, nay, they cannot, break away.

On the occasion of my second visit to the Siva shrine beyond Conjeeveram, it looked as deserted as before.

The large, recumbent bull some paces in front, had a broken nose and its high pedestal was at the disposal of many clambering children at play. However, this morning a Brahmin stood, as if waiting and expectant, beside the huge iron gates, heavily padlocked to bar out intruders. When he saw me get out of the car, he at once produced a key and threw them open; then guided me into the courtyard. I asked him to show me the Kurumbers, the object of my visit, and he seemed to hesitate, but then retraced his steps and near the tank I saw them sculptured: little men with curious, high caps, short sticks and gourds over their shoulders.

Evidently that was not all! The priest took me back to our starting-point and then to the left side of the temple, where a few, wide, stone steps led to a pillared, stone chamber. He went up and beckoned to me to follow, but stayed my steps from crossing the threshold, having ushered me thus far into the Presence. It was evidently the Hall of Audience.

Facing me in the high, dimly-lit chamber sat the gods, side by side: figures about four feet high, robed as if for a reception: Siva with a crown of beaten gold; Parvati, his wife, with the glitter of it and jewels in the folds about her neck and bosom.

An eerie feeling took possession of me, that I had been brought there for some purpose: had been commanded, that the gods might look at the white woman from the West, who had come to visit their golden city.

Utterly taken aback, confused at being thus confronted by them, I lent myself to the Hindu conception—with a faint wavering belief that something else must surely happen and transfixed by the stony, hard stare that met my eager gaze. I stood quite still . . . waiting . . . but they made no sign.

Motoring away, I could see across the plain the high towers of a huge, irregular pile, of which no two walls are parallel, standing out grandly against the blue of the sky: yet another temple of the "Lord of the One Ether," as Siva is designated in Conjeeveram.

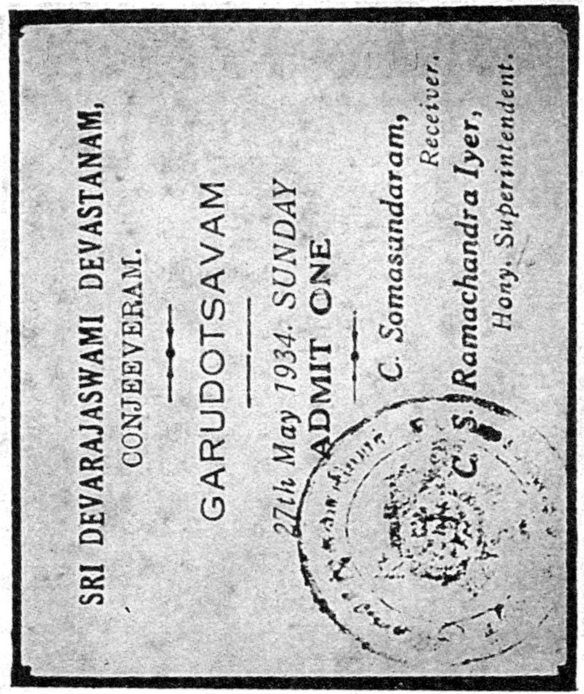

SRI DEVARAJASWAMI DEVASTANAM,
CONJEEVERAM.

GARUDOTSAVAM

27th May 1934. SUNDAY
ADMIT ONE

C. Somasundaram,
Receiver.
C. S. Ramachandra Iyer,
Hony. Superintendent.

INVITATION TO BRAHMIN KITE FESTIVAL

It is to this temple that Vishnu rides, on one or other of his vehicles, during the ten days of the Grand Festival, and here in the holy of holies, is preserved one of the five most sacred *lingams* in the whole world. Made of mud, for that is one of the chief constituents of the universe, it is frail with age, held together by a wire and never washed as others are. A point of flame burns eternally before it in the dim recesses of the sanctuary.

This great and important pagoda is probably one of the oldest in the town and had so small a beginning that legend associates it with a mango, the tree that bears fruit for the gods. In its architecture is the impress of Buddhism, which was the prevailing creed in Conjeeveram until the seventh century. Though King Asoka's stupas have all been swept away, Hinduism, with its powers of assimilation, has thus preserved memories of the faith, which was a Kshatriya [1] revolt against the arrogant pretensions of the Brahmins and an appeal for better living:

> "To cease from all sin,
> To get virtue,
> To cleanse our own heart,
> This is the religion of the Buddha";

and again:

> "The real treasure is that laid by man or woman
> Through charity or piety, temperance and self control,
> The treasure thus hid is secure, and passes not away.
> . . . This a man takes with him."

When the new Hinduism asserted itself about the middle of the seventh century, it had absorbed some details of the dying creed and found a place for the Lord Buddha in its Pantheon of Gods, as the ninth incarnation of Vishnu.

In Conjeeveram, the Lord of the One Ether, "whose *lingam* represents the God of Life and Death with such irony, yet with such perfect truth," reigned unquestioned for centuries and there still are one hundred and eight

[1] The Warrior Caste.

shrines dedicated to Siva in the city, whilst Vishnu dwells in only eighteen.

It was in the eleventh century that the philosopher, Ramanuja, led a vigorous campaign against Sivaism, when Gunda Gopalo Rao was governor, who vowed a temple to Siva's rival, if his wife, who was barren, should bear him a son. This came to pass in due season and with the material of a demolished Sivaite shrine, over a cave where lived a demon, was laid the foundations of the Vaishnava temple in the south-eastern corner of Vishnu's golden city, that is now by far the most important in all Conjeeveram. For the community is the wealthiest in the city and Vishnu is the rich man's god, who enjoys ceremonials, processions, precious gifts such as the necklace presented by Lord Clive and firework displays on festival nights.

The temple area is surrounded by high walls and its gate towers, called *gopurams* though not so high as Siva's, are extraordinarily effective, opposite to one another with an oblong court between, and a small tank with water as green as the sea. All the buildings are of comparatively modern date and the dwelling of the god is marked by three large golden balls gleaming in the sunlight.

Probably the oldest of all is that attributed to a Raja of Vijayanagara, who beautified the temple in 1515. It is a sculptured hall; a *mantapam* of a hundred pillars supported by curious mythological creatures, upright on their hind-legs. Here, little Vaishnava boys are instructed in the tenets of their faith, having around them lovely carvings of the *avatars*, the incarnations of Vishnu, to aid their memories. Ten of these are officially recognized, but with the astonishing elasticity of Hinduism, the numbers have stretched to thirty-nine.

One corner of the larger court, shaded by a sacred *neem* tree, is set apart for a collection of upright slabs carved with serpents and stone images of many-headed cobras: creatures that are dormant until summer comes; therefore symbolic of resurrection; the sleep and the awakening. Ananta, the "Endless One," encircles the earth and is a symbol of Vishnu and of eternity: on Sesha, that has a thousand heads, he reclines during four months of sleep. Vaishnavas bow as they pass the serpent enclosure and there are special festivals for snake worship connected with the desire for fertility and long life. Hindu high-caste ladies may be seen with their silver vessels beside a long ant heap in the secondary court, midway between the gate towers. They pour milk into the holes to feed the snake that is said to live there, though never visible. If within a month a snake should bite some member of the family, it may be killed with immunity: its life forfeited by its ingratitude.

Vishnu is truly the family god and every housewife worships his attributes, the *Salagrama* and the *tulasi* plant, that are to be found in all orthodox Vaishnava homes. The one is a black stone, preferably an ammonite, that may be converted into an image at the will of the worshipper, for the god dwells within it. The other, holy basil, is most carefully tended and watered in the backyard and at night a tiny lamp burns at its foot. "In its roots are all the sacred places of pilgrimage, in its centre are all the deities, and in its upper branches are all the Vedas."

The caste mark is like a three-pronged fork, and is emblematic of the three Gods of the Trinity, Brahma, Siva, Vishnu. It appears at intervals on many walls of the temple precincts: the two outside lines are painted white or yellow, the central one red: and on our lord the sacred elephant in the processions. When I saw him first in his stall near the great tank, he was motionless and so much the colour of the walls, I thought him carved in stone.

Ramanuja's adherents are distinguished by a connecting streak on the nose.

The philosopher, who taught that life is a manifestation of God, has a shrine all his own in the grounds and many followers, but there are dissentients, who preach another system of philosophy. His code insists on the concomitancy of the human will: that of his opponents, that there can be no salvation save by divine grace. In the picturesque phraseology of the East, one sect is compared to a monkey whose cub clings to its parent for help: the other to a cat that seizes its kitten to hold it in its mouth and save it from all harm.

The two parties have been known to fly at each other's throats during the Grand Festival, but I was told it would be pessimistic to expect any desperate strife over their philosophy since they came to an amicable arrangement, by which one sect precedes the god in his royal progresses and the other follows him.

At all events, it must have been a great triumph for Ramanuja to place his own particular deity at the head of affairs as the Supreme Being in Conjeeveram, where he is worshipped under the title of Varadaraja, "Kingly Giver of Boons." In his entertaining guide to Chingleput District Mr. Venkatesan tells us that "the whole festival is designed to illustrate the admitted superiority of Vishnu to Brahma and his complacent patronage of Siva."

There is a large population (of which 75,000 are Hindu) in the sacred cities, and many a *choultry* and rest-house for pilgrims; but even so, thousands have had no roofing but the summer sky. They poured in from every direction and by every possible means of conveyance: rail, bus, bullock carts and *jutkas*. The evening train from Madras, which habitually takes three hours to cover forty-five miles, was late by yet another three. It was long past midnight, when the mass of humanity it carried unpacked itself at the journey's end.

This I heard at the Ramakrishna Dispensary, where I spent my mornings to see the god pass by in state, in one guise or another and always on a different vehicle. The *Math* is a charitable institution, one of nearly a hundred mission centres in India, and elsewhere, for educational and medical work and propaganda. They are the result of the new Hindu movement, which called for Voluntary relief workers towards the end of the last

GOPURAM OF THE SHRINE AND MARRIAGE MANTAPAM AT VARADARAJASWAMI TEMPLE

century. Its founder was Swami Vivekananda and I remember that he came to London and was received by Canon Wilberforce, Moncure Conway, Mrs. Annie Besant and others who concerned themselves at that period with orientalism, religion and ethics. The community was joined subsequently by Miss Margaret Noble who, as Sister Nivedita, worked wonders for the cause and wrote delightful books, *Cradle Tales of Hinduism* and *The Web of Indian Life*. They idealize existence and religious belief in India out of all recognition by less poetical minds, for she seemed to see life always as it ought to be. Would that it were so!

During festival week the *swamis* most kindly placed the use of their portico at my disposal, and whilst I sat waiting there, they expounded to me the philosophy of their founder, Swami Vivekananda.

"Some here are miserable for your and my salvation, so that we may serve the Lord coming in the shape of the diseased, coming in the shape of the lunatic, the leper and the sinner. . . . Why should you go to seek for God—are not all the poor, the miserable, the weak, Gods? Why not worship them first?"

As the *swamis* explained to me, their philanthropy is not that of the West, born of a desire to please God, but because God is Himself manifest in the poor and suffering, they give them aid.

They took me over their house—excepting only into the shrine, where I might not enter—to a large reading-room with newspapers on its table and English books on its shelves and the lecture hall hung with coloured prints of many Hindu divinities. There was always ample time for conversation as I had to make my way to their house in Nellukara Street before the sun's rays beat too fiercely on my head and to escape the crowds that gathered there later in the vicinity of the *Math*. It was admirably situated for my purpose on a high bank, that runs along one side of the wide road with houses atop, at the corner where four crossroads meet to form a large open space where the god's bearers were often stopped amongst the masses of the devotees that had congregated to do him honour.

A marvellous scene this, of shifting colour like a kaleidoscope, with a background of copper-coloured men against which the *saris* of the women almost blazed, so gorgeous were their hues in the radiant light. The weavers of Conjeeveram are famous and have their special quarter in Siva's golden city, where may be seen strands of red and gold and green and blue silk, newly dyed, stretched and pegged along the footwalk, waiting to be wound and woven. Here is the description of a young unmarried girl's dress, that I chanced upon in an Indian story I was reading at the time:

"She wore a Conjeeveram silk *pavadar* with broad, pink silk borders and a silk gown of light blue colour with frills and flounces stretching up to the elbows. Her waist was encircled by a gold *oddeanam* with gold bead pendants under which her gown was gathered."

We were awakened every day after sunrise by a salute of three guns that nearly shot me out of my bed. It notified to the world of Conjeeveram that the god had arisen, was being washed, dressed, anointed and perhaps also fed to sustain him during the many hours of his slow progress through the golden cities.

"Prepare ye the way of the Lord!" A huge *tom-tom*, beaten almost continuously, filling up a bullock cart, heralded his coming: the sacred elephant, dignified, slow moving in scarlet drapery to the ground: the sacred white horse on to which fond parents hoisted their little ones, for to ride a few paces on it ensures good luck.

Beneath the shade of a ceremonial umbrella, mounted, at his first appearance, on a sacred peacock of dull, silvered metal, Varadaraja himself in his character of "Smiling Benefactor" carried on a raft borne on men's heads!

The Day of the Kite was still more exciting, as a special function was held at the temple. I have a card of invitation, on which this favourite mount is depicted as half eagle, half man. He is the king of birds with a white face, red wings, gold body and he feeds on snakes.

Many more pilgrims came into the town. One large company of men and women in canary-coloured robes and with long hair passed on to a village thirty miles away, where they sacrificed their clothes and their locks to the god in the hope of offspring, and the women also their chastity. A few days later I saw them returning with shaven heads and half-naked. Any child that might be born to a woman after her pilgrimage would be accepted by her husband as his own child.

On the third great occasion, the god made his appearance in the guise of a beautiful wanton. For this manifestation vague reasons were given which I could neither understand, nor accept; being perfectly aware it was illustrative of a debauch. The gods can do no wrong and are devoid in the minds of historians and worshippers of any human ideas of decency, or morality.

After sunset, when Varadaraja had been put to bed, *tom-toming* began again and every evening there was a procession in honour of some village, or minor deity. The god of the sun and an image of the moon god would come out for an airing and to enjoy the firework displays which cost, it was said, seven hundred rupees. It seemed to me at the end of a fortnight that the quantity had been unlimited for even that amount of money.

I could not discover whether Kamatchi, the "Loving Eyed" wife of Siva, ever makes her appearance in public; or if she really returned to her fine temple after she fled from Conjeeveram, together with Siva and Varadaraja, in the reign of the iconoclast, Haidar Ali. The three of them were carried away like corpses, attended by funeral processions, to the jungles of Trichinopoli District and report says that the Raja of Tanjore took possession of the Loving Eyed One, for she was all of gold. Who, then, was found to play her part as goddess of wealth and pleasure, for there are many devotees at her shrine on Fridays seeking her favour?

When the British had broken the Muslim power and the Hindus were thereby enabled to worship their idols again with immunity, the other two exiles ventured to return. The Lord of the One Ether came back to his temple in the charge of a Brahmin, and "In 1799," says an inscription on a pillar, "Lallatandra Mallaji . . . caused the idol Varadaraja to be brought back from Udayarpalayam to Vishnu Kanchi. May blessings attend!"

In the late afternoon of the sixth day of the festival, I went into Little Conjeeveram to see the car made ready that would be the god's vehicle on the next two days. It looked enormous, dwarfing everything in its vicinity, and had a crimson canopy draped over the shrine. Life-sized statues of Vishnu in wood support the enclosure and a wooden charioteer ostensibly drives four prancing horses that paw the air. The whole structure rests on tremendous wheels and is dragged by means of cables of rope many inches thick. It needs a thousand men to move the car.

In the days of long ago, there were always sufficient volunteers willing and ready to fall into line. Then it became the monopoly of the weaver caste to have this honour, who were rewarded by a gift, a gold chain, for their own god. Two years ago, they grew lazy and tiresome. Traffic was held up in the city for days, for Varadaraja in his car had come to a standstill at this corner, or in that street, and could not get back to his home again. The weavers were replaced by the lowest caste of *Sudras* and this year the Government insisted on a guarantee of four thousand men under a threat of prohibiting the car procession altogether. It is thought and said for these reasons that the car festival "is slowly dying: let it die!" But would that be wise?

To see the ponderous vehicle, I had taken a short cut to Little Conjeeveram through the grounds of the Scotch Mission Hospital, but I made my return journey from the temple, as the car would make it, from the entrance thronged with fruit sellers, flower sellers, *Sadhus* and beggars.

At first the street was narrow, lined with little houses close against each other and cupboard shops: then widened where brass ware was displayed and there were shrines and banks. Then came the quarter of the Potters, a large Hindu School, the *Munsiff's* Court and Post Office till I reached the corner, that turns one way into the splendid thoroughfare of Raja Street and the other towards the *Math* where I would await its coming next day.

The air was stifling: the leaves hung limp, half dead upon the trees and I hoped that the god would choose an early hour to go forth amongst his votaries and spare those who must drag his car under the noontide sun, whose fierceness might be safely prophesied.

For day after day, a greater god than Varadaraja, "Vasudeva, Supreme Principle of Divinity," [1] copper coloured, drove his seven steeds through a brilliant heaven and their colours were gorgeous as the hues of the rainbow, disseminating Unit Rays of a blinding light and heat. Each Unit Ray has within it the possibilities of the solar spectrum.

It was nearly midday when the car reached the *Math*, for the stars and astrologers had decided that it could not leave the temple before eight, the "auspicious" hour.

No wonder the two priests in attendance on either side the god, who was invisible, found it necessary to fan the charioteer on his lofty perch, as he pulled up his prancing horses at the corner of the square, and the thousand men, who were dragging the car, had a few minutes' respite from their exhausting labours.

"Do you think," I said to the *swami* at my elbow, "that God is really in the car?"

He looked at me in surprise and answered: "If he were not in it, there would be no merit in dragging it along."

To acquire merit! That is the dominant reason for every act of faith or works. Nay, more than this. From the mouth of Vishnu himself comes this couplet in Sanskrit:

[1] *Surya-Siddhânta.*

"If for my sake thou sinnest, it becometh merit:
All merit without reference to me becometh sin."

The salute was fired. With immense difficulty and the help of leverage at the back "the four-wheeled image car, more than thirty cubits high" started on its way again: the god accompanied, as always, by rows of Brahmins chanting the Vedas. Arrogant and supercilious gentlemen: sleek and fat as well they may be since they are fed throughout the time of festivals at the expense of the temple authorities. They were naked to the waist, save for the sacred cord of three threads of cotton twisted to the right, worn over the left shoulder to the right hip, whose investiture requires the adoration of the sun. "Let us contemplate the divine splendour of the sun-god, the donor of bliss to all: that he may give us every kind of happiness in the World," is their *mantra*. They should have been bareheaded had not the Supreme Principle of Divinity been blazing too fiercely even for them; but the *swami* remarked upon it, nicely sheltered under the portico and swathed in his monastic draperies of apricot pink.

Only once I saw a *devadasi* with her elegant, swaying movements amongst the immediate votaries of the god.

The crowds closed up behind the car to follow it along Raja Street to Siva's temple. It would have been easier to walk on their heads than on the road, or footway.

I did not go again. Prostrated by the heat (the thermometer at F. 108), I stayed in the bungalow for a few days and looked out from the verandah at processions passing the far corner of the road from a temple near by of Vaikunta *Perumal*, with, or without, the ten-headed cobra beside her, under another umbrella.

From her ancient sanctuary came the insistent, sinister beat of *tom-toms*. Other instruments added to an increasing volume of sound, until one night I thought her votaries had gone quite mad.

At last I was driven to invoking Indra, god of rain: "Master of Waters, come!"

"... The blazing sun was veiled
Behind a sheet of clouds. A mad wind hurled
The boughs of helpless trees from de to side,
And falling leaves in fierce concussion whirled
In crazy circles on the dusty ground,
Bewildered and gyrating round and round.

. . . .

Lightning flashed across the angry sky:
Thunder rent the air, and torrents swept
Upon a startled world . . .
the raindrops leapt
Upon the steaming earth."

PADMINI SATTHIANADHAN.

CHAPTER IX

SHADOWLESS

"A curious mixture of care and neglect, of extreme finish and what is left undone, of refinement and barbarism—a décor without a soul."
J. AND J. THARAUD.

"Born in that circle where they can only fulfil the lot marked out."
SISTER NIVEDITA.

IT is a night's journey from Madras to Tanjore, and when I wakened in the dawn and looked out on the surrounding country, there was more water and irrigation to be seen than I had yet met with on my travels. It is the sacred Cauvery River and the rich alluvial soil that have gained for the district its names of Garden of South India, and Granary of the East; though this may be, after all, a mere matter of comparison with an aridity of long stretches of seemingly uncultivable land elsewhere, that filled me with dismay.

Whenever a town was reached, this feeling was quickly succeeded by one of delighted surprise at the wide roads: so different from the conception of town planning in the Near East, where streets are narrowed into corridors and houses nearly meet across them, built for shade. Now I realize that it is a consequence of religion: that wherever Brahminism flourishes and there are splendid temples, there must also be spacious thoroughfares, where the god can make a royal progress on his favourite vehicle.

To this Tanjore is no exception, for Hinduism has been firmly established since those prehistoric days when Vishnu killed the giant Tanjan and granted his dying request, that the town should be called by his name.

It would seem, therefore, that the Shadowless Temple, in the Little Fort, should hallow the Beneficent One,

THE SHADOWLESS TEMPLE, TANJORE

the Preserver, but it is not so. Siva is worshipped under the title of Brahadeswara Swami, the favoured deity of the Emperor-builder Rajaraja and his commander-in-chief, who superintended its construction with the aid, it is said, of a Hollander. Long colonnades reaching out from the principal shrine contain the phallic emblem; a count of one hundred and eight succeeding each other in close proximity, for that is the numerical value of certain Sanskrit letters, beloved of the gods and known to the initiates in his worship. Above this lengthy array of *lingams*, crude frescoes are painted on the walls in vivid colours of other deities, the many-headed cobra and the story from the *Puranas* of the sixty-four miracles attributed to Siva.

Facing the temple tower is the god's celebrated vehicle, the *Nandi*, which began to grow after it was placed couchant in its fine stall with painted roof. The huge, monolithic bull of black granite was already sixteen feet long by twelve feet high, in its recumbent position, and this gave cause for grave anxiety, lest the *mantapan* would soon prove too small to hold the creature. Someone had the inspiration to drive three nails into it: one into its head, one into its hump and a third into its haunch, where the wounds made may be seen on close inspection. This drastic treatment proved effectual; the *Nandi*, frightened, grew no more.

The tower above the shrine is a miracle of laborious carving like all these strange pyramids of Hinduism. It is surmounted by a block of granite weighing eighty tons, brought to the elevation of over two hundred feet by means of an inclined plane, which had its beginning in Scaffold Hollow village about four miles away.

On the south wall is a commemorative, sculptured portrait of the Dutch architect, but legend disputes this and declares that the figure was intended for an Englishman and was prophetic—so far back as the eleventh century—of future British domination. The bearded face under a wide-brimmed hat reminded me of our King Hal who had Tudor ideas about the ruling of a country, well suited to impress the Oriental mind. It is notoriously characteristic of Hindus that they are indifferent to a choice of masters. "What does it matter to us," says an age-old proverb, "whether Rama administers the country, or the giants?" And Rama had been the founder of the dynasty of the sun, the hero who had attained divinity! For ninety per cent of the population this is as true to-day as it was nine centuries ago, when was built the Shadowless Temple.

It is the people who have given it that strange, uncanny name. "How can there be a shadow when there is a crown on top?" said my old guide, discussing the reason of it with me, at an hour when the title was certainly quite justifiable. The tower stood up against the skyline, so grandly and proudly self-sufficient, and every gleam of sunlight was concentrated on the golden spire, that marks the shrine of Siva: there was not a shadow to be seen.

Unlike most other temples of South India, the temple of Tanjore was built entirely in one reign and on a definite plan, that was military in its conception. Its surrounding, protective walls are ancient fortifications enclosed by a deep moat, so that the entrance to it is over a small bridge and even a portcullis is suggested, that is not there: only two gate towers beyond, one ninety feet high and the second about sixty. Here it has the appearance of a fortress: the impress of the priest is less obvious in its architecture than that of the kingly warrior, who caused its building. To a stranger, there is an absence of concealment, obscurity and horror more often met with, and the Tanjore temple seems less hopelessly engulfed in the lowering, black shadow of Brahminism.

"The Brahmins are of the worst," said the well-known missionary, Schwartz, close friend of the last reigning Raja Sarabhoji. "When they have obtained a district they flay the people with unrelenting and inhuman cruelty and with the most philosophical sangfroid."

It saddened me to see in the Christian chapel built to the good man's memory, tablets with English names of pioneers who, in the service of the East India Company, had borne the burden and heat of the day and had helped to lay the foundations of a great Empire, that is being ruthlessly hacked to pieces and swept away by Empire breakers.

Between the Schwartz chapel and the sacred Sivaganga tank with its muddied waters, outside the southern gateway of the Little Fort, I watched a Hindu woman at her prayers. She was walking round and round and round a magnificent and holy Arasu tree twenty-one times, on a narrow platform that encircled it at a height of about seven feet, ornamented with *nagas*, serpent images presented by childless Hindus. This perambulation together with *puja* at a small shrine should be repeated for twenty more successive days that she might eventually give birth to a son. Snake worship, the most ancient faith of all, is persistent and undying, assimilated by Hinduism after the Aryan immigration into India.

But of the cult of Kamatchi, the Loving Eyed One, whom the Raja of Tanjore had rescued from exile in the jungles of Trichinopoli, I heard not a whisper and saw nothing at all. Yet the golden goddess must have been housed by him in the rambling, ancient palace within the great Fort, for her safety in those troublous times of iconoclastic Muslims; during the hammer-handed rule of Haidar Ali and Tippu, who forcibly enrolled Hindus amongst the followers of the Prophet.

Rumours must eventually have reached Kamatchi of peace throughout the land and religious toleration: of a new Raj which had not only saved, but protected the gods. Did she perhaps slip away one night through the palace gates, from a host reluctant to part with a golden treasure, and find her way back to Conjeeveram, to the temple that bears her name? Or is she still lying hidden somewhere within these fast decaying walls? In the temple-like *gopuram* of stucco, ninety feet high, that is now the armoury? Behind a panel, or a painting, in the Durbar Hall, where Raja Tulzaji, in his curious, triangular turban, received his courtiers, or pronounced judgment from the long platform of black granite where once was his throne?

Assuredly not in the famous library, the finest in South India, for that was dedicated to the goddess of learning, Saraswati, who would not tolerate a rival amongst the Sanskrit manuscripts, eight thousand of which are written on dried palm leaves. In these ancient books kings are represented as receiving guests with the question: "What have you seen elsewhere?" When they depart, "What have you noted here?" Of Kamatchi there is no record, which is passing strange. Vainly, I peered into small shrines near the entrance to the *zenana*, only to catch a glimpse of a gnome-like figure painted red, or a hideous black Ganesh.

This was in the third quadrangle of the palace: the two outer ones are deserted and the spacious apartments in the buildings round them are closed and empty.

Tulzaji died in 1787 and his half-brother, who succeeded him, was set aside for an adopted son, Sarabhoji, to whom is due the fine collection of books in the Saraswati Mahal. After twelve years he signed a Treaty with the East India Company, by which he handed over the State to them in exchange for a suitable provision for himself and his descendants, some of whom are still pensioners of the British Government and resident in the palace. His son, Sivaji, had no male heir, so with him even the titular dignity came to an end. There is left now a ghostly kingship, a white marble statue of the last Raja on the platform of the Durbar Hall with its crude decoration of Hindu gods, painted in bright colours, by whom witnesses swore to having spoken only the truth. Retainers make their appearance in the quadrangles on occasions, as a last semblance of royal state, when strangers are expected.

It chanced that the Rani's second daughter had her fourteenth birthday celebrations during my brief visit to Tanjore. Then, in the outer quadrangle, the car was stopped by a sentry and we were passed on from one servant to another until met by our hostess on an upper

NANDI MAHARAJA

storey at the threshold of her apartments. The three ladies, mother and two daughters, are *purdah* like flowers in a hothouse, that may not breathe the outer air.

The elder princess is married and much occupied with her baby girl of about a year old. Her attire was very simple, as was also the Rani's: they were the desirable dull background for the heroine of the festivities, who blossomed like a rare exotic, an eastern rose. Her *sari* was crimson with a deep border of bright green and her whole person glittered with gold and jewels from her banded filigree headdress to a multitude of anklets and of rings upon her toes. In her ears rubies sparkled and through her nostril was a catch-pin from which depended a beautiful large pearl. Ornaments clasped her throat and necklaces hung about her, half hidden by a garland of the red roses and jasmine of Tanjore. One of them alone was worth a king's ransom in gold pieces, just smaller than a *louis d'or* and strung so closely that they overlapped each other.

[I held my breath and wondered, as I examined it, how much of Kamatchi had gone to the making of that long necklace of gold coins without alloy.]

So heavily weighted by her grandeur was the youthful princess, that we had to leave her, poised and solemn as an idol, against the dark background of a high, carved blackwood chair; whilst we walked through rooms and endless corridors, that seemed devoid of comfort, or of care. It was as if the household were all just moving out of them, or had only just come in.

Originally the palace had been five storeys high, but the top one, now derelict and unsafe, is being slowly demolished and has no roofing but the sky: a dreary place of promenade, with the rare diversion of looking on at a match played in the tennis court far down below.

Before leaving, the little round brown mark of a twice-born, a Brahmin, was impressed on my forehead by the Rani and my hands filled with flowers and betel nut daintily encased in green leaves tied with gold thread.

The joy of living seemed terribly curtailed for these

three gentle princesses, but to the Oriental woman brought up in a cloistered atmosphere, ill educated, married before she is fully grown physically, or mentally; there is a certain compensation in the hothouse feeling of superiority to wild flowers: a prestige in being always sheltered from the common herd. *It is the custom of our people:* that suffices.

How fortunate too is their position, compared to many others, as wards of the British Government that safeguards their material welfare. "Most Indian women, especially *purdah* ladies, are terribly helpless as far as legal matters are concerned," says the Maharani of Baroda. "When it comes to a question of property management, many are content to let men have the entire control and so women have been swindled out of considerable fortunes" . . . "Some hesitate to consult a male practitioner . . . by reason of *purdah*."

" What of India to-day? The half of the entire nation is paralysed. Women have not freedom like men," said Swami Gnaneswaranandaji, in his lecture last October. "We move slowly if we move at all."

Purdah is a hopeless barrier to progress. Though these women also possess votes, as an experienced woman legislator has pointed out, "unless they have the goodwill of their men, they will not be allowed to exercise their votes."

Many of them have not the slightest wish to do so. The Hindu ideals of procreation and domesticity are deeply rooted in their minds and Sister Nivedita has told us, truly enough, the prayer of the average Indian wife.

> "From the arms of husband and sons
> May I pass to the feet of the Lord."

Age-old traditions and customs of which the palace of Tanjore is a tragic museum and of a bygone Oriental splendour. The substance has vanished with the years: only a frail shell still remains, that is crumbling to pieces and will soon be shadowless.

CHAPTER X

THE CULT OF MINAKSHI

"I know the vice that is going on to-day in all the great Hindu shrines, but I love them in spite of their unspeakable failings."

Mahatma Gandhi's Ideas, C. T. Andrews.

"I do not disbelieve in idol-worship."

Gandhi.

. . . .

"I walk in a dreamland that is peopled by giants and shapes of terror."

India, Pierre Loti.

My first drive through Madura was sufficient to convince me that here was no ordinary city, quite apart from the fact that "from time immemorial it has been the political and religious capital of the extreme south of India."

All I knew of its history was troublous: of the destruction of the outer wall with fourteen towers and a magnificent temple by the Muhammedans in the thirteenth century. Only the two shrines of the principal deities were spared, probably from a superstitious dread of the invaders that the wrath of the gods might be visited upon themselves.

A serious effort to grasp subsequent details has ended in defeat. It is such a long and bewildering record of chiefs, viceroys of the Vijayanagara Empire, rulers weak, or strong; of exhausting struggles due to disagreement about succession to the throne; of internal strife; of tribal warfare with Tanjore, Travancore, Mysore, Tinnevelly, the Tiruvada Country; of anarchy in Ramnad; of a struggle for Hindu independence of the Muslims; and lastly, of an unfortunate co-operation with these religious antagonists which, in time, had disastrous results. I was thankful when the British appeared on the scene to put an end to such hopeless confusion and to learn that they restored peace and order and quieted the whole District in 1783, under Colonel Fullerton.

Then I turned back the pages to the chapter on Tirumala Nayaka, whose reign was rendered illustrious by "works of magnificence, truly royal" and who made a dream city of his capital.

He was the eighth viceroy in direct descent from Nagama Nayaka, a trusted official of the Raja of Vijayanagara, who appointed him administrator of this southern province of the Empire, when it was at the zenith of its glory. At that time the feudatory states could depend on their overlord for help and protection, if need arose, and for this they paid annual tribute. In the course of the next century, the position had changed; the strength of the Empire had waned and its glory; whilst Madura had become powerful and its rulers ambitious for independence from a yoke that galled.

When Tirumala came to the throne in 1623, he at first pursued this policy of his predecessors with infinite tact, trying to humour the Emperor by sending him gifts, hoping to escape thereby the payment of a regular tribute, whilst acknowledging him as his suzerain with the utmost respect and deference. It was a relationship and situation too ambiguous and delicate to be lasting, but for a time it had partial success.

The ambitious and quasi-independent viceroy needed the money for so many purposes; more especially for the defence of the realm, no longer assured by the overlord, and it was exasperating to pay out to him at least one-third of the revenues of the country for no practical advantage whatever.

Hitherto Trichinopoly had been the capital of the kingdom and Tirumala continued to hold his court there for many years after his accession. Some time after 1640 he transferred it to Madura. To live in the heart of his dominions must have eased the administration at a period when travelling was slow and difficult, even for

THE KALASAM, MADURA

Rajas, and other means of communication absolutely nil. He certainly made one prolonged tour throughout his territories, which is recorded in an inscription of 1652, and to have a more central point for departure must have been almost essential. It was safer also to be at some distance from the war zone, with hostile states around his own, and to have the barrier of two forts, Trichinopoly and Dindigul, both of which must fall before an attack could be made on the new capital.

From that time forward, any surplus revenue was devoted to the works of architecture, that have survived him as a memorial through the centuries, to prove how great a man he was, "the strength of whose arm was hard to be resisted . . . whose enemies ascended high mountains as soon as he climbed on his mighty elephant, who surpassed the enemy of the ocean in attacking a town for conquest." It is of greater moment to us of this generation that he was an artistic genius.

Though, towards the end of his reign, Tirumala adopted the unsound policy of joining forces with his hereditary foes, the Muslims, of which they were quick to avail themselves for their own benefit; he was driven into it by the exaction of the tribute, which was an injustice. He was severely taken to task for his disloyalty by the King of Mysore; that he, a staunch Hindu, should prefer to ally himself with their common enemy, rather than join the Hindu League. No one could then foretell the happier days in store for all Hindus and Muhammedans alike, after the conquest by the British.

That tribute Tirumala would not pay. In him throbbed the pulse of splendid living that demands great wealth, and his colossal palace that is a manifestation of his character won my admiration by its grandeur and simple dignity. It is entirely unlike anything Hindu, and I welcomed the absence of hosts of exuberant statues of men and beasts that are expressive of patient, unremitting labour, that is not always art. The Jesuit Fathers sought for a parallel in Thebes, but surely it is more reminiscent of Saracenic architecture.

The principal apartments surround a courtyard that is one hundred and sixty feet long and one hundred in width. There are spacious corridors on three sides with lovely Moorish, foliated arches supported on giant pillars ornamented in *chunam* shell peculiar to Madras and for its fine, white, polished surface. The palace, strangely enough, might have been intended for a mosque of the Prophet. It has three domes, one of which lights the lofty throne room surrounded by galleries on an upper floor, that repeat the design of the arched corridors.

Here, on ceremonial occasions, were seated Tirumala's two hundred wives, that were the stumbling-block to his conversion to Christianity (said the Jesuits), who nearly all, and certainly the most distinguished amongst them, were burnt on his funeral pyre with him, when he died.

The Fathers failed to realize that his protective attitude towards themselves and his lukewarm toleration were due to an enlightened outlook, rare at that period, and not because "he never had the courage to accept the consequences of his conviction" that their faith was superior to his own. He had no such conviction, nor did his policy towards them differ from that of the other Nayaks of Madura.

Writing on this subject, a modern Indian historian of the Viceroys has said:

> "The services rendered by the *Nayaks* to Hindu religion and culture in weathering the storm of Christian missionary propaganda, without resorting to an organized policy of persecution, are not sufficiently appreciated. But for their unremitting care for, and love of, Hinduism and for the bold fight they put up in defence of their national ideals, the cause of the age-long civilization might have been jeopardized."

Thanks then to the religious fervour of the Nayaks, Madura has remained a very citadel of the Hindu cult: its temple ceremonies are indeed age-old, practised for thousands of years before the Viceroys ruled the province, in comparatively modern times, for the space of about two centuries.

Never a more pious Hindu than Tirumala Nayaka! When he transferred his capital from Trichinopoly, it was said that he did so out of love for the ancient seat of God, Sundareshwara, the title by which Siva is worshipped there. The Chronicles state that only the gods of Madura could cure him of the disease of catarrh from which he suffered: it was for that reason he made the change. Certainly his relations with them were both intimate and excellent, and no wonder it was so, when he bore them constantly in mind. To his piety is due the lovely and picturesque country club, known as the Tank of the Raft, three miles outside the busy town, where all is still and deserted as if a spell of silence had been laid around this unique pleasure house of the gods. It is a phantasy of art: a beautifully-carved pagoda set on a square island, in the midst of a huge tank and embowered in greenery; high trees embrace and threaten to hide it out of sight. At each of the four corners is the daintiest pavilion imaginable to do service as a shrine. Parapet of the tank, pagoda and shrines are outlined with ten thousand lamps on the night that the temple deities are brought there for a floating festival and drawn round the island on a raft.

The Lord Sundareshwara consented to leave his dark cell in the temple and deigned to invite himself for a ten days' visit every year to the Viceroy, provided that Tirumala would build a guest house for him worthy of his presence. It was begun at once: the *choultry*, that is such a magnificent creation and cost one million pounds, but alas! was never finished. The god's pillared hall, where he would have rested, has been turned into a *bazar*, but as it was not consecrated, it has at least been spared the ignominy of whitewash.

Its gateway faces the eastern and principal entrance of the great temple; the third largest in South India, its precincts and buildings cover fifteen acres. It is stupendous and fascinating, but its mysteries and furnishings are illustrative of a people whose minds are steeped in primæval horrors. How impossible to describe its four lofty *gopurams*, endless corridors and arcades and *mantapams*, its Hall of a Thousand Pillars!

The two principal shrines are noticeable from afar off by their golden coronals: Sundareshwara's on the north; the other, on the south side, dedicated to Minakshi, his "fish-eyed" spouse. She was renowned as the local deity long before Siva, god of the Brahmins, set foot in Madura to dispute with her possession of its people's faith.

Before the days of the Nayaks, there reigned over the province a dynasty of Pandya kings, and one of them, Pandian, closed the temple of the goddess Minachiamman, which infuriated her and she determined to punish him for his wicked boldness. It happened that the king had no child and so greatly desired one that he thought of adopting a little girl, whom he found one day lying in the palace. She had a curious bracelet on her arm, exactly like one worn by his wife. However, the astrologers warned Pandian that she would bring evil to him and his house, so he had her put into a basket and thrown into the river. The wise men had guessed that she was Minachiamman, incarnate in this form, seeking vengeance. Being a goddess she did not drown, but was picked out from amongst the reeds by a merchant, who brought her up as his own daughter.

About this time Siva was also incarnated as a merchant, and hearing of the mysterious origin of this young girl, he was so interested that he sought her out and took her to wife. After some years they became very poor, till, at last, one day he insisted on taking her strange bracelet to Madura to sell it, though she begged him not to do so. He was at once clapped into prison for theft, for the king's wife had just lost her bracelet and the two of them were identical. When Minachiamman heard of her husband's arrest, she assumed the form of Durga, the demon goddess, and she slew the Pandya king. Having once tasted blood, she has never lost her craving for it and must be constantly propitiated, lest she give that awful cry: "*Main bookhi hoon!*" "I am hungry: I want blood."

This folk story is extraordinarily interesting, for it illustrates the methods adopted by the Brahmins in assimilating pre-Aryan worship with their own creed, though some of the details of the legend probably originated with a palace intrigue. They found the cult of the demon goddess firmly established at Madura, and they effected its union with Hinduism by marrying Minakshi, the "Fish-Eyed" to the Lord Sundareshwara. There is no doubt that, to this day, she has maintained her supremacy and is the predominant partner, although Siva assumed nominal sovereignty after the nuptials had been celebrated. Ten days in every month are set apart to do her honour.

* * * * *

It was late in the afternoon when I entered the vestibule of the temple at the eastern gate and leisurely examined eight colossal, gaily-painted statues of my friend, Lakshmi, that upheld the roofing at either side. Each figure is lady president over some source of wealth, and to have so many, within a comparatively small area, must be of great assistance to the trade carried on behind them in booths, that fill the space between these unusual pillars and the walls.

Above the heads of the Lakshmis are depicted scenes from the life of the temple deity, Minakshi: her fight against Hinduism, her marriage with Siva; the assumption of his sovereignty by the god; and the birth of their son, Subramanya, who was afterwards appointed by his father, god of war.

Presently a voice behind me said, "I am a Brahmin of this temple. I advise you to study the miracles of Siva painted on the walls of the arcades, round the lotus tank, especially for the benefit of pilgrims."

I turned to thank the priest for his instruction and found myself fronting the sculptured guardians of the temple, on either side the entrance of a market hall: and also two enormous and horrible black figures, Ganesh to the left of me, Subramanya on my right. Smoke and scent of camphor and incense rose from the trays attached to them, constantly replenished by the pilgrims.

The day's trade was nearly at an end: vendors of coconuts, sacred clay in balls and slabs, garlands and offerings for the gods, were resting from their labours: some had closed down for the night.

I walked through slowly, my bearer following me, a Catholic of the second generation and a much-travelled Hindu. When we reached the entrance to the sacred precincts, surrounded by an arch of one hundred and eight lamps just lighted, the temple attendants turned him away—a Harijan. As a "foreigner" they gave me permission to go in and I went on alone, almost to the heart of things.

To reach the arcades of which the priest had spoken, I had to pass through a small *mantapam*, lined on either side with statues of the gods: Siva in various forms, Vishnu, in his *avatar* of Krishna, playing the flute. This led to the Tank of the Golden Lotus. Its waters, in an unruffled calm, mirrored no reflection of the buildings which encircled it, so strangely dark in colour and glutinous from the honey and *ghi* with which the *lingams* are anointed daily and washed off into this thrice holy bath for pilgrims. They were seated, or lying about in groups, or singly, against the pillars, and there were many *sanyasis*, robed in apricot, begging from the solitary stranger. Some were dead asleep. No one seemed in the least interested in the miracles of Siva, that I had been sent to study; but the light had failed and they were not seen easily, despite their crude and vivid colouring. Yet I lingered awhile at the corner where I found them to follow, with pleased eyes, the long lines and perfect proportions of the cloisters and the wide, stone steps around the sacred tank.

At last I turned to the left and walked on until I reached the parrot *mantapam*, where beautiful green birds,

GUARDIANS, ENTRANCE OF MADURA TEMPLE

imprisoned in small cages, expiated by proxy the sins of the pilgrims, who had presented them as offerings to the temple, by a lifelong captivity within those grey, stone walls. There was a lovely white cockatoo on a perch, with yards of heavy, steel chain attached to one foot. It had been there, it is said, for twenty years.

I walked on again and found myself in the Hall of the Thousand Pillars, whose sculptures are said by experts to surpass those of any other in their marvellous elaboration.

Within the enclosure of the last fifteen of these splendid columns, I found myself at the shrine of Minakshi, the "Origin of all that was, is and will be." In this outer court was a mass of human beings, mostly male; but also there were a few gentle, quiet-looking Brahmin women with flowers in their perfumed hair. We wondered mutually, they and I, what had brought us into this strange galley?

Facing the entrance of the mysterious sanctuary was a railed-in gangway and at its head a raised bas-relief of Siva, dancing. Placed below this, in a line on either side, were grotesque highly-coloured puppets from a life-size doll show.

Almost immediately opposite, just beyond Minakshi's shrine, a temporary platform had been set up for Kali, the worst manifestation of Siva's wife; a repellant figure in a blood-red robe, holding a long spear and with her foot resting on the prostrate body of her spouse.

I turned away from it, rather sickened, only to face another huge black image of Ganesh, said to have been found during the reign of Tirumala Nayaka, when the Tank of the Raft was being excavated.

To the left of the elephant god was the passage of the tower, that separates the temple of Minakshi from the temple of the Lord Sundareshwara. I went through and found myself in an enormous pillared hall, where a death-like silence reigned and monolithic elephants kept guard of the entrance of the god's sanctuary. A solitary light burnt within it: he must have been asleep.

Conveniently near by was a *Nandi* and a gold-plated flagstaff that passes out through the roof. I was then attracted by a cage in which nine large discs represented the planets and the nodes, placed at short intervals round a copper-coloured sun. A little farther on I came suddenly upon a black, horrible, gigantic Durga; her breast and left arm were bespattered with the *ghi* flung through the bars of her cage in which she was imprisoned like a dangerous beast. This had been done by relatives of those she had stricken down with smallpox.—"I want blood."

The atmosphere was heavy and noisome. I fled into an outer court where I had already seen four ancient fluted pillars, that had been excavated. Each curve of the surface emitted a lovely sound when struck by any stone one might chance to pick up. Melodies from a remote past floated out from them; weird, beautiful harmonies of other days, some other temple, other gods than these.

On this night, uncanny shapes pervaded the quadrangle. In the fading light, so near darkness, they were hardly discernible. It was occupied by a company of Hanuman's army: monkeys swarmed along the ramparts and the *gopuram*. They had come in from their own green mansions without the temple walls, attracted by tit-bits given to them by the pilgrims, who were playing with them, their sacred pets.

The temple bell ringing for service at Minakshi's shrine recalled me there, but I halted, perforce, between two huge pillars of Sundareshwara's hall, where I was sheltered from the crowd. But not from the musicians, who, seeing a vacant space near by, took up their position close to me, and their loud, insistent, strident notes and the beat of the *tom-toms* hammered on my brain.

I turned my back on them just as the *pujaris* were carrying out the smaller idol that represents the demon goddess in processions and a shimmer of gold and jewels in a palanquin that was shoulder high, flashed past. The whole of the surrounding scene was lit up by

TANK OF THE GOLDEN LOTUS MADURA TEMPLE

flaring torches and the litter was preceded by the chief priest, naked to the waist but for his sacred cord of the twice-born Brahmin. Other priests followed the deity, holding up round baskets for offerings from the dense crowd, and from Minakshi's outer court poured forth a riot of copper-coloured flesh; of dark brown faces lit up with frenzied zeal, arms and breasts and foreheads smeared with the sacred clay, or white ashes, and the blood-red sign manual of the cult, stamped like a seal athwart the three lines of Sundareshwara on the brow. Like a surging sea, they swept across the *mantapam*, past Siva's shrine, neglectful of, unheeding the god of Hinduism, to a *nautch* of the *devadasis* in the outer court, which they refused to let me see.

After thousands of years she still triumphs, Minakshi —Kali—Durga, Origin of Evil.

CHAPTER XI

A MARRIAGE OF THE GODS

"Here is seen the holy place in the great ocean which is well known as the *Setubandha* [1] and worshipped by the three worlds. This is extremely holy and destroys great sins. Here formerly the Lord Mahadeva (Siva) was pleased to show favour to me."

RAMA *in the* "*Ramayana*."

"At the beginning of the construction of the *Setu* Rama established Siva known as Rameswara and worshipped him."

"*Adhyatma Ramayana*."

"Rama is one-half of Vishnu."

THERE is no doubt that of the material benefits conferred on mankind by an emotional religion, the immigration of pilgrims from all parts of the country to holy places in a desert and nearly uninhabitable region, has been most useful. It relieves the congestion of crowded cities, more especially in the unhealthy season, and brings life and money and work where there is none and the few aboriginals would otherwise starve. More often than not healing waters, or a salubrious climate, can be added to the alleged miracle, and those who wish to purify their souls may also alleviate, or cure, the diseases of the flesh to which their sins may sometimes be ascribed.

Were it not for the epic poem of the Ramayana and the miracle of the bridge built by its hero to transport himself and his army to Ceylon from the mainland, who would come to Ramnad District, to this barren strip of shifting sand dunes, a dreary waste with scanty vegetation? How wise were the Rajas, the pious "Lords of the Causeway," to build the fine temple of Rameswaram in honour of Rama and his worship of the Siva *lingam*, enshrined in its chief sanctuary. It is one of the few

[1] Adam's Bridge.

places of pilgrimage, which attracts men of all religious sects in India. Rama, the national hero, himself raised to the dignity of a god, is an *avatar* of Vishnu and votaries of both the principal deities of Hinduism may worship there.

Only a few miles distant is a confluence of two seas, which has a strange, occult significance to Oriental minds. It is enjoined upon the pilgrim that he should go there first, remain for a month and take three dozen baths. What better advice could the gods give for hygiene and health? He must primarily address himself to the demoness, who guards the meeting of the waters and who is a "terror to the world": beg her acceptance of sand and crude coloured palm-leaf ear-rings before he dare enter the calm pool of the Bay of Bengal, where it is protected by a narrow isthmus from the tempestuous Indian Ocean.

After the baths at the *Setu* and the worship at Rameswaram the fortunate pilgrim may hope for absolution from all his sins, protection for the future in his journey through life and salvation at its close.

It was at this point, called Danushkodi, that Rama broke the bridge with his magic bow, that had been Siva's, and posterity therefore has no evidence of the miracle of its building, except that due to faith and remembrance of an epic of the third century B.C.: golden days of minstrelsy, when it was sung to the melody of some stringed instrument by disciples of the poet.

Long, long ago there lived a king in the north of India who had two sons, Rama and Lakshmana by his first wife and a third, Bharata, whose mother prevailed upon her old husband to instal her son as his heir and banish the eldest to the forest for fourteen years, by means of "that great and occult influence, which is one of the few rights of half-savage womankind."

Rama, the dispossessed, was married to Sita, who adored him and whom he had won as a prize at the court of her father, the Raja of Behar and Tirhut to bend the magic bow of Siva. The princess would not forsake her husband, nor would his brother, so the three of them went forth into exile in the Vindya mountains.

The poor old King, unhappy and repentant, died of grief, and Bharata refused to step into Rama's shoes. He went off in search of his stepbrother and tried to persuade him to return to the kingdom, that was his, and assume the reins of government. But he found him adamant in his purpose of carrying out their dead father's decision. "How could he fight against the decrees of Fate which had destined his brother to the throne and himself to the forest?" Then Bharata went back alone to Ayodhya and reigned there in Rama's name, and never once did he issue an order without first saluting the rightful King's shoes, which he had brought away with him.

The banished trio had wandered about for ten years when they met a sage, who advised them to live at Pancavati on the Godaveri; but they found that the neighbourhood was infested by demons and staying with the friends, on a visit, was Supanaka, sister of Ravana, the celebrated ten-headed demon-king of Ceylon. She fell in love with Rama, who would have nothing whatever to do with her. Thereupon she appealed to her friends to avenge her, who were all servants of Ravana, for whose destruction Vishnu had become incarnate and was born into this world. The demoness, further, played upon her brother's feelings and drew such a vivid picture of Sita's charms, that he became inflamed with desire and determined to abduct her.

By their wiles the friends arranged that Rama and Lakshmana should both be absent from the cottage together, drawn off by a deer and only an ancient vulture left on guard. The bird fought to protect his mistress and succeeded in wrecking the king of Ceylon's aerial car, but Ravana carried off Sita in his arms.

When the brothers returned and realized what had happened, Rama nearly went crazy with grief and rage at his misfortune and threatened to destroy the three worlds. "These mighty beings [the gods] also were

CORNER ENTRANCE PASSAGE, RAMESWARAM TEMPLE

subject to the control of Fate, and of them also no man could say that unmixed happiness had been their lot."

According to the legend, Ceylon, or *Lanka*, was in those days seven hundred miles distant by sea from the mainland, but, nothing daunted, Rama and Lakshmana started off for Ramnad District and arrived at its southernmost point, where is now the dreary little sanatorium of Mandapam. An ideal spot for an absolute rest cure far from the madding crowd, that passes by unheeding on its way to the holy places; a relief from the stuffiness of Madura and rock-heated Trichinopoly, both within easy reach of the bathing and delicious breezes, that blow in softly from a bay sheltered by three islets, just visible on the horizon.

Leaving Mandapam, the pilgrims have the curious experience of being out at sea in the train. An aqueduct connects it with Rameswaram Island, along a line of reefs, by the Pambam Channel. Waves beat against the iron piers on both sides, and in receding before their next attack give glimpses of the dark brown living coral in the ocean. Stray pieces are picked up and sold in the temple as sacred to Sita, who used it—so the women pilgrims say—for painting caste-marks on her face.

No doubt there have been geological changes along the coast since the ancient days of the Ramayana, but it must have been somewhere in this neighbourhood that its hero providentially met Hanuman and his army of the "Third Root Race," half men, half animals. He formed an alliance with their King, Sugriva, and was joined by monkeys and millions of bears who, when they had arrived at the sea, threw mountains into it, uprooted trees for the embankments and bridged over seven hundred miles of the ocean in five days.

Whilst the *Setu* was being built, "Rama established a *lingam* of the Lord Mahadeva (who loves to wear the elephant hide), in the middle of the *Setu* and worshipped him."[1]—"If thou art pleased, O Lord Sankara! stay

[1] "Kurma Purana."

thou here for the purification of the world and for the good of men." [1]

When these terrifying cohorts landed in Ceylon, they found themselves a day's march from Ravana's capital, which was set upon a hill. The gods appeared to Rama to inspire him with fresh courage for his task and sprinkled him with holy water for, as Vishnu, he had been appointed by them to slay the ten-headed demon-king. Here we have an allegory of the inter-caste struggle between Brahmins and Kshatriyas for equality, which in another century brought about the rise of Buddhism. A Brahmin, Ravana, defeated and slain by Rama, a Kshatriya.

Tradition in Ceylon places the last scene of the contest between them at a submerged place not far from the south shore of Colombo, where pilgrims go out in boats to worship the warrior hero.

Flushed with victory, Rama sent for his wife to tell her that he had removed the slur of dishonour from her name; but that his self-respect would not permit him to take her back, after so long a residence in another man's house. Sita, who had suffered torture and starvation to preserve her chastity, defended herself with great dignity and with bitter tears, so that the monkeys wept aloud to hear her. She asked for her funeral pyre that she might end her life, but Brahma appeared to announce that she was Lakshmi, the heavenly spouse, and the god of fire lifted her out of the flames to the arms of her husband.

Reconciled, they flew away in an aerial car to Rameswaram, that Rama might show her the route that he had taken with his army. He broke down the *Setu* in three places, and first of all at Danushkodi, with his magic bow and destroyed it, that Ceylon should never be invaded again.

Brahminism did not accept defeat at the hands of Rama, the Kshatriya. Popular tradition asserts that he was obliged to establish the *lingam* after, and not before, Ravana's death as a penance for his sin of *Brahmahatya*.

[1] "Siva Purana" (Canto 31).

However that may be, the first Lord of the Causeway, Sethupathi, Raja Sahib of Ramnad, was installed by him as Protector and crowned on a sacred stone still preserved in Ramnad Palace. This family have been vice-gerents of Sri Rama since those prehistoric days, guardians of the emblem and now of the Rameswaram Temple.

According to tradition, the *lingam* was at first enshrined in a thatched cottage in charge of a *Sanyasin*, and the oldest portion of the temple of dark, hard limestone unlike the rest, was built in A.D. 1173 by Udaiyan Sethupathi with the help of a Raja of Kandy, who sent over enormous stone slabs, forty feet long, that are in the central colonnade called "The Magnificent."

Although, from being built in sections and added to from time to time, much of the beauty of this great structure is wasted, because it is inadequately displayed, such part of it as I was allowed to enter impressed me more than others I had seen. "It is the Dravidian style in its greatest perfection." A "foreigner" is not admitted to the inner colonnades, but I seemed to walk on endlessly through spacious, superb and lofty corridors, always with a vista opening out before me of still more and more fine pillars wonderfully carved. The total length of them is said to be four thousand feet. At times I could have thought myself in Egypt.

It is natural that there should be restrictions on the sight-seeing of Europeans in the holy places, but visitors who comply with regulations may be assured of courtesy and a kind welcome from the temple treasurer.

The gods, Siva and Parvati, are worshipped under the titles of Rameswara, or Ramanatha, and his consort Parvadhavardhini. The goddess holds a *durbar* every Friday evening at nine o'clock after the usual service, when a master of ceremonies calls for recitations from the *Vedas* and the Tamil *Thevarams*. After this, she proceeds in her gold palanquin to the shrine of Ramanatha and is carried round it three times to the chanting of Vedic hymns. A procession escorts her with priests in advance of it who perform *puja* at certain appointed places of its route. Musicians follow with pipes at full blast and *tom-toms* loudly beating and the *devadasis* give their dance. When all is over the divine pair are carried to their swinging gold couch in the bedchamber and the doors are closed for the night.

During August, the month of the Marriage Festival, Parvadhavardhini held a special reception on the first Saturday in the forenoon and I preferred to go to it rather than on the preceding night, as I wished to see the temple at its best in the glorious sunshine.

A small image of the goddess, hung with many garlands, was carried through the corridors and into a pillared hall decorated in white and silver for the marriage ceremonies which last seventeen days. On this morning she was also expected to make a progress through the town in her gold palanquin. Standard bearers awaited her departure and two sacred elephants that would precede her to clear the way. One of them, in passing, demanded an offering from the stranger, and when I placed a rupee on his trunk, curled it round and passed up the money to the *mahout*.

When the goddess had left with her retinue I had an opportunity of seeing the vehicles used by the different deities inhabiting the temple, for there are minor lights beside the two shining ones, and on specified occasions they take the air on a silver mouse, or peacock, or a swan; or else on the gold lion, or the Divine Cow. For great festivals a splendid silver car has been built of recent years that cost eighty thousand rupees.[1] It is fitted with electric bulbs, so that at night innumerable jewels blaze in a silver setting and make of it a veritable fairy coach for Siva and his Consort.

I returned to Rameswaram on the fourteenth night of the festival and first of the wedding ceremony, which took place in the Kalyana *Mantapam*, directly facing the temple of the divine bride. The invitation was for seven o'clock and as I passed through one of the side corridors to take my seat, I had a glimpse of the bride and bride-

[1] About £6,000.

groom, each in a litter covered with garlands and surrounded by a throng of votaries clapping their hands in joy and raising them in adoration of their gods, palms and finger-tips pressed together in the attitude of worship.

The marriage hall was lofty, long and rectangular in shape, with wide corridors beyond the high pillars that supported the roof and had stiff, huge, gaudily-painted figures standing out from each column in bold relief just above one's head. Electric fans fluttered a cloudy sky of white crêpe with silver stars and festoons of many-coloured silks hung from this improvised ceiling.

At the upper end on a dais was a magnificent marriage shrine, large enough for two people, roofed and draped in ruby and silver, its ends hung with garlands infinitely long of scarlet and white flowers. The floor was carpeted with crimson and placed upright on it, side by side, were two large, embroidered cushions for the bridal pair to lean against.

The whole of the ground space of the hall was covered, without an inch to spare, by countless men, women and children; the two sexes separated by a narrow aisle in the middle, for the passage only of one person. Across it, facing my armchair, was a rosebud garden of women in bright-hued *saris*, and at my feet rows upon rows of copper-coloured bodies; arms and brows smeared with white ashes. Twenty thousand pilgrims had come in on the previous day for this marriage.

It was a strange scene, unequal in the disposition of wonderful and sombre colour, the whole brilliantly illuminated by hundreds of electric lamps.

Presently there was a brief uprising of the mass of votaries, for the gods had arrived in their litters; the bridal pair that are all of gold and cost their worshippers five thousand guineas.

The priests formed up close to the shrine and there were temple women near it, when Siva and his bride were lifted and placed in position against the pillows. A blinding light blazed above their heads, gleamed on precious metal and still more precious gems.

The service began: a ceremony of slow, mysterious, inexplicable movements, one priest succeeding another at the shrine; a passing to and fro of silver, sacrificial cups and a platter; a strange instrument waved about the bride's head; incense burned before them both.

So the hours passed by with continuous music of pipes and beating of *tom-toms*, and would again on two succeeding nights to end, until another year, the "Holy Marriage Festival that is worth worshipping" at the Temple of Rameswaram; a sacred place known also as "The City of the Gods."

"Mandura and Saduragiri mountains are turned as it were into two pillars for the suspension of the swing, Mahameru and Ponmalai are converted into beams; the powerful *Sesha* has made itself into two cords, the tree of wisdom itself which shines supreme is turned into a plank; Vishnu and Brahma hold the cord and sway the swing to and fro; the learned Vedic Brahmins stand near and perform the necessary rites; the beautiful Goddess Parvadhavardhini is at your side. Swing softly."

[Song of the *devadasi* at the door of the bedchamber.]

ROCK TEMPLE OF SIVA, TRICHINOPOLY

CHAPTER XII

TEMPLES

"Les caractères généraux de toute architecture théocratique sont l'immutabilité, l'horreur du progrès . . . la consécration dés types primitifs. . . . Ce sont des livres ténébreux que les initiés seuls savent déchiffrer."

VICTOR HUGO.

"An impure and degrading fetishism."

FERGUSSON.

SUNSET and the beautiful glow of evening over Trichinopoly! Below me, an immense plain like a vast green sea of vegetation and waving palms that high winds sweep through to bend and reform their crests again. They caress a strange mass of stone on a high rock; a prehistoric monster fossilized to granite carrying on its mutilated back a temple and in its breast the soul of this Hindu city.

Under the *kalasam*, a golden coronal, is the seat of the people's god; there reigns the ancient cult of Siva, as immutable, unchanging and nigh as old as the Rock itself, a belated birth-pang of nature after the creation of the world.

Men burrowed into the heart of it, contrived a succession of stairways, giddily steep, through covered passages to landing-stages, and explained the reason of their labours in frescoes to commemorate a legend, senseless for all but the initiates of their extraordinary creed.

The god's wife, Parvati, is depicted as very human indeed, nearing the time of her confinement and anxiously expectant that her mother may be with her in the hour of her delivery. But her poor mother is stranded on the farther shore of the Cauvery River when in flood. She stands alone and helpless, an aged peasant woman with a bundle on her head, unable to cross the turbulent waters that overflow the banks after the *monsoon*.

Then it was that Siva assumed her shape to console his wife, presided at the birth, washed the infant and kept up the illusion until the river subsided and the real mother was able to make her appearance on the scene. Again he transformed himself into a god and has been worshipped on Trichinopoly Rock ever since as Matrubutheswara, "the Lord become Mother." Pilgrim women come there in their numbers, with an offering of flowers in their hands, and climb the three hundred and sixteen steps to the apex of the Rock, for they think that so understanding a god as this will surely grant them the supreme gift of a child.

On my arrival I found a little crowd awaiting me and the temple elephant in the courtyard saluted in anticipation doubtless, in his proud position as doorkeeper, of some small fee. From one landing to another I was carried, like a goddess, in a luxurious chair by bearers, who set me down to wonder at the frescoes; at another stage, to look at the properties required for the festivals; at a pillared *mantapam*, and on the fourth floor for a glimpse into the dim recesses of the shrine. After that, to my content, we emerged into an open space to view the lovelier handiwork of nature from a small pavilion, where Siva is brought once a year for an airing. Still visible was a temple "salutation of the threshold" on the pathway of the god. Here a processional road runs round a hump of the Rock and from the farther side I saw the Cauvery river gleam in the dying sunlight, winding its way, snake-like, through the land.

In sudden conflagration, the aftermath illumined the gold-topped covering of the sanctuary; then, as suddenly, died down: it was the salutation of the night.

Little wonder is it that the plain is fertile and green barley is upspringing, since much blood has been spilt there of white and coloured men on one of the chief battlegrounds of Southern India. After Tirumala Nayaka's death, Trichinopoly became again the capital of Madura province, with a princely residence built partly out of materials taken from the great Viceroy's beautiful palace at Madura, but a poor place by comparison. Then followed a lengthy history of intrigue; alternate Hindu and Muhammedan incursions; of warring States; British and French troops on opposing sides; Hyder Ali's invasion and his terrible son Tippu laying waste the island of Srirangam, and at long last, an enduring peace under British rule in 1801.

In those days of strife the temples became fortresses and the British had a powder-magazine covered with hieroglyphics in the Pallava caves of the Trichinopoly Rock Temple.

As for the splendid earthly residence of the Lord Vishnu, at Srirangam, approached from the mainland by a picturesque bridge of many graceful arches over the Cauvery River, it was desecrated by the presence and brutalities of Tippu, the Tiger.

This temple, dedicated to the god in his aspect of Ranganathaswami, is the largest and richest of South India: its jewels and plate are most valuable and include a gold salver, presented by King Edward, when he visited India as Prince of Wales. It has seven enclosing walls with streets and houses and shrines between, and harboured an immense crowd, taking cover from the Muslims in 1790, behind forty-feet monoliths and carved *gopurams*, at least three times higher. The Brahmins, only, had access to the inmost courts around the central shrine of the god and the *pariahs* bore the brunt of the attack in the largest one outside the rest, with its splendid, still unfinished gateway, built of enormous blocks of stone.

Within is a narrow flight of steps and a platform extending for a long distance, from which one looks over a collection of buildings and shrines, that resembles a nest of boxes, fitting closely inside one receptacle just large enough to contain them all. The plan is more curiously Eastern in conception than beautiful and not impressive, except that such a vast area is covered by extensive temple precincts and *mantapams* with a very small sanctuary in the midst, around which the rest of the assemblage must have grown up gradually.

Beyond this platform of the outer court no Christian, Muslim, or Harijan may pass, and there is a notice board on the wall to that effect. Besides, the atmosphere seemed to me charged with hostility; but it may have been due to my impossible request that I might be present at the forthcoming festival of the god, for which I had timed my arrival at Trichinopoly.

"You can't attend the procession," my friends had said, in horrified surprise, "it would be dangerous."

My guide at first pretended that I had mistaken the date, but when cornered, told me frankly that he would be boycotted by all his friends if he accompanied me to the temple after the god had left the shrine, where he is jealously guarded by the caste Hindus.

That he was leaving it in August had astonished me, since it is a well-known fact that in the third week of July Vishnu falls asleep for four months during the rainy season, only turning once on his side in the middle of September. Then, why this sudden activity in which I might not share? Why should he be wakened from his slumbers?

For it is at Srirangam that, swathed in many draperies and garlanded, he habitually reclines on the coils of the five-headed cobra, the emblem of Eternity.

* * * * *

Hindu temples generally are paired: one rises in honour of Vishnu and it is straightway incumbent on the votaries of Siva that a shrine be erected to their god in its immediate vicinity.

So it is at Srirangam. Opposite the Great Temple and under half a mile away from its *gopuram* and enclosures is another famous place of pilgrimage, established by the Sivaite community, over a perennial spring. The precincts and surrounding walls are smaller, probably older and said by Fergusson, the great authority on

THE LORD VISHNU AT SRIRANGAM

Indian architecture, to be more beautiful than its rival. It was impossible for me to form any opinion, for just now Jambukeswaram is hidden by much scaffolding and ladders, and the courtyards are ankle deep in dust. In the first of these hangs a signboard that explains its curious name. It is a picture of the *lingam* enshrined in the sanctuary, under the shade of a rose-apple [1] tree, that is greatly venerated, and the figure of the god's consort, Parvati, appears in the right-hand corner at the top.

Here also, as at Srirangam, I was made to feel myself unwelcome and that Hindu temples and Hindu cults had not been established for the likes of me.

[1] Jambuka.

CHAPTER XIII

HINDU AND MUSLIM

"Tippu destroyed tanks everywhere; he never built one."

VISCOUNT VALENTIA.

"It has been a real sorrow to me to see lately in different parts of India, great clashes over the externals of religion, showing, if they show nothing else, a tendency to pursue the shadow rather than the substance."

H. H. THE MAHARAJA OF MYSORE, *April* 6, 1927, *when re-opening the Mosque built by his grandfather for the Muslims.*

HARDLY had I left Trichinopoly, with recollections still fresh in my memory of the vegetation and green grasses upspringing round about the great Rock Temple, than news came through that the south-west *monsoon* had failed, the crops were ruined, prices of grain and rice——the food of the people and their animals—had doubled.

In Bangalore, also, the weather was astonishingly hot and sultry for the end of September and we too began to study the sky daily and anxiously for seasonal rain to refresh the drooping plants, that no amount of artificial watering seemed to satisfy; and to fill once more the irrigation tanks and wells, that were alarmingly empty. Clouds would gather in the late afternoon, disperse, gather again, perhaps to send us a brief shower and only make us long for more. It seemed as if the north-east *monsoon* were failing also and the horrid spectre of famine stalking over the plateau began to haunt its Indian inhabitants, whilst the Government considered measures of relief. Already cattle were being driven in from the district to be sold by owners, who could no longer feed their beasts.

It is at such times of stress that the Brahmins come to the rescue of the people, bid them cease their panic and put their faith in Indra, or Varuna, the rain god.

"Have mercy on us thy poor children," they prayed, from the first day of October, when hope had failed them; and began their ceremonies; Vedic invocations with the accompaniments that the West recognizes in terms of "sympathetic magic."

The priests urged that in 1904 and again in 1918, when drought threatened, their rites had proved entirely successful and they asked for two thousand *rupees* [1] with which to carry on their *puja*. An influential committee was formed of well-known citizens, Indian officials and public men, with a retired District Judge as chairman. Donations poured in, especially from the grain merchants, and sacrificial offerings were made by the Brahmins to the sage Rushyasrunga, long since dead, for wherever he had dwelt there could not be a drought. It was for that reason King Dasaratha, of legendary fame, brought him to his kingdom of Ayodha to inaugurate for his people an era of plenty.

Other Brahmins stood daily, for six hours at a time, breast deep in water, chanting special Sanskrit hymns. In an adjacent *math* yet another group recited verses to propitiate Agni, god of fire, seated round a blaze kept burning with pure *ghi*, whilst the sun god flamed in the heavens and drove piercing, hot rays into the hard-baked earth.

"After twelve days," they predicted, "it will rain." In the meantime, I had left the plateau on a visit to Mysore City, eighty-seven miles distant, and had travelled through a stricken, thirsty land.

On my arrival, the air was cold and excessively damp, the pavements still drenched and shining with moisture in the lamplight: greetings were prefaced by "Look, how wet it is underfoot, we have had heavy rain!" which was significant of what the tension had been.

So all was well with the world of Mysore. The Brahmins did not seem to be troubling themselves about Varuna and the *monsoon*: nor did they need to do so. It poured every day; too much for the pleasure of a

[1] About £150.

visitor like myself, and presently the wall of my barber's sister's house tumbled down and a bridge was washed away. Then I began to wish that the Bangalore folk would cease their incantations, for it was not yet the twelfth day and if this weather continued they must soon reverse the order of their going; fill a huge, earthen saucer with pure *ghi* and set a cotton wick alight in it to float upon the waters, whilst they murmured prayers against a heavy flood.

Since April, however, the Sunwheel has revolved through six hot, dry, lunar months of summer, and though we are now at the turn of the Hindu year, it is not yet very perceptible. The Cauvery River, which flows through the State, along the borders of Mysore Plateau, for one hundred and fifty miles, is too low at this juncture for even a thought of trouble from an overflow of its sacred waters. They have brought such priceless blessings to the people, it is no wonder that they worship their river and deify nature in visible shape, as a goddess bestowing magical gifts. I have visited her shrine at Sivasamudram, where her sculptured figure, in flawless black stone and always garlanded, stands in a niche of the western wall of a great dam. It is suggestive of the earth-mother, the matron of early middle life, and her peaceful countenance faces the Sun of dawn. Her hands are filled symbolically. She has four, that she may hold a lotus flower, for love; a rosary of prayers; and two sacred vessels with *soma*, the moon-plant from which was extracted the elixir of the gods and a continuous stream of water, indicative of her beneficence. Though the magnificent Gersoppa Falls, of the Sharavati River, at the north-west corner of the State, bordering on Canara, are more famous for their wild, grand scenery and said to be the finest in all India; yet they have most surely been surpassed by the blessings the cascades of Sivasamudram have showered on the heads of the people of Mysore.

About a thousand years ago, with much labour and considerable skill, their ancestors had contrived a system

Tamil Brahmins of South India

of irrigation by means of bridle-works, which are still useful over an area of nearly two hundred square miles; but the reservoir Krishnarajasagara dam, constructed in 1911, capable of storing 44,827 million cubic feet of water, has nearly abolished the terrors of drought and any necessity for Vedic ceremonies in honour of Varuna. This, more especially, since the completion of the Irwin Canal, which carries water northward from the dam, into the arid districts of Maddur and Mandya. The Canal supplies water for forty thousand acres of land, and the sugar-cane industry, which resulted from this enterprise, though of quite recent development, is already a source of wealth. A wise Administration is endeavouring to interest the young men of this generation in the study and pursuit of agriculture, as one means of solving the problem of unemployment amongst a class of would-be copyists and clerks.

The Krishnarajasagara dam, second in size only to those of Egypt, was but a consequence of other gifts born of the Cauvery River and the science of Europe and America combined. Its object, originally, was to render more efficient and extensive the plant at the Kolar Gold Mines, in Bowringpet District, which never ceases working day or night. Air compressors, tube mills, pumps, crushers and winding engines had all been controlled, since 1902, from the first Hydro-Electric Power Station installed in India at Sivasamudram, ninety miles distant. In the summer months the supply of water ran dangerously low and there was an ever-increasing demand for power, that could only be met by storage. The surplus from the dam has brought water to the houses of the people and has given them that other boon of civilized life—light. There are seven electric installations now. No more filling of buckets from some deep, ancient well; no more greasy, smoky, ineffective oil-lamps; but a continuous flow of pure, filtered water out of taps close to the hand of the housewife, and the cupboard shops of the *bazar* brilliantly lit by innumerable electric bulbs and the mere touch of a few knobs on the walls. Magic gifts! Miracles of the Falls of Sivasamudram, the goddess Cauvery and the vast, calm lake that is called *sagara*, the sea, motionless as if enchanted.

It is a curious fact, that Tippu Sultaun had the idea of building a dam across the Cauvery in 1792, but all that materialized of his project, apparently, was a stone tablet, inscribed in Persian, to commemorate his laying of the foundations on a day when there was a lucky conjunction of the planets. "The start is from me," said Tippu, the "Bestower of Gifts" as he called himself, together with many other titles, "but its completion rests with God." Not with his God and Mahomet the Prophet of God, but after a century and more with the God of the British and the Goddess of his Hindu victims, every trace of whose rule he had tried systematically to destroy. The stories of his cruelty to the Royal Family of Mysore and to the British, who were prisoners in the terrible dungeons of the Fort at Seringapatam and fettered; of the officers who were compelled to drink poison and the English boys who were circumcised and enslaved are too well known to bear repetition. The world was well rid of such a callous wretch and the only excuse that can be made for him, that he was mentally deranged; so mad that he could not hold the kingdom his father had bequeathed to him.

The 4th of May, 1799, was an "inauspicious" day for Tippu, of which he had been forewarned by the Brahmins and his own Muhammedan astrologers, so he spent the morning in propitiation, giving them valuable presents: an elephant, buffaloes, a black bullock, a black goat. In vain! before nightfall he was dead.

The assault of the British and Sepoys had been ordered for the hottest time of the day, when the enemy had fed, was somnolent and unprepared—the Sultan himself had just finished his midday meal, when he realized the attack and buckled on his sword. As he crossed from the outer rampart he was wounded by a musket-ball, and again when half-way through the arch of a gateway.

A grenadier, attracted by his gold ornament, seized his belt and another ball struck his right temple, so that he fell lifeless, amidst a mass of his own followers.

On the next afternoon his generous foes, British and Hindu, gave him burial with every mark of respect, and all the honours due to Muslim royalty, in the beautiful mausoleum he had built for Haider Ali and where his mother, also, had been buried. Some of his people "prostrated themselves" before the body wrapped in muslin and covered with a rich brocaded cloth . . . and expressed their grief by "loud lamentations" and later showed their somewhat misplaced loyalty by a tablet on his tomb:

"The light of Islam and the Faith left this world; Tippu became a martyr for the faith of Mahomet. The sword was lost. The offspring of Haidar was a great martyr."

As if in confirmation, when night fell, a terrible storm raged in the heavens, so that some were killed and injured. Nature's dirge when a Great One passes out.

The mausoleum and adjacent mosque are built on a wide terrace above the land, where rounded cupolas and pinnacles and minarets stand out in dead-white purity against the eastern sky. Waving feathery palms, in close proximity, have shot up beyond arcades with their pillars of polished serpentine and balconies above, as if wishful to outstrip the highest points of decorative Muslim art. Where once were *fakirs' choultries* and scenes of suffering and despair of wounded men, now there are woods shutting in this lonely, peaceful spot.

Of Tippu's splendid palace within the Fort, there are but ruins for landmarks, but his two-storied summer pavilion, outside the precincts, "Wealth of the Sea," is a harmony in lovely colours. Every inch of wall space within is covered with gorgeous arabesques. In the verandah are two large, amusing frescoes which depict the vainglorious Sultaun sniffing at a rose, exultant at the defeat of the British at Polilore, near Conjeeveram, and Colonel Baillie carried past him in a litter. Masses of troops stand at attention around this scene and there are gun-carriages, chariots and horsemen wildly galloping anywhere.

When Seringapatam became the capital of Mysore State, in 1610, it must have been a beautiful city and unique from the fact of its insulation. It is an island of the Cauvery, three miles long from east to west and a mile in breadth. Even in those days it was already very ancient, for it was said that Gautama Buddha worshipped Ranganatha Swami in the temple, where I might only look into a wall shrine at its entrance, to see a black image partly covered with a red rag; a replica of the Hindu god within the sanctuary.

In Tippu's time there were many such pagodas, and he added stately Muhammedan art and architecture; his fine palace set in wonderful gardens, Haidar's tomb and the Great Mosque which is standing to this day close by the inner Bangalore Gate of the Fort.

When the odious Sultaun was safely in his grave, the gratitude of the Mysoreans to the saviours of their country knew no bounds, and the Maharani Regent presented Seringapatam to the British in perpetuity. But the island proved too unhealthy to be Garrison Headquarters and the military authorities handed it back again ten years later and removed the troops to a smaller area in Bangalore, the present Civil and Military Station.

This, surely, was an exchange of territory from a grateful people to their protectors. The military authorities considered they had the right to sell certain portions of their property from time to time to private persons, who hold British Deeds of Title. Their wishes and that of the large Indian Community, who are mostly descendants of Tamil settlers, are trifles of no consideration to the Government of India, whose policy makes it important that Mysore State should enter the Federation.[1]

* * * * *

[1] "Retrocession of Bangalore," *Indian Empire Review*, Dec., 1934.

It was eventide, when I sat in the car outside Tippu's Mosque near the *maidan* that had been a parade ground, where small boys were finishing a game of football; watching the cattle being driven home and goats, and all the other sights and sounds that said clearly the day's work was done and over till the morrow. Little, twinkling lights appeared in the minarets and presently the voice of the crier called his co-religionists to prayer. "There is no God but God," he told us, yet a few yards distant the car was stopped by the ringing of a temple bell. We drew up by the road-side whilst a procession passed of Ranganatha Swami, one of three hundred and thirty million gods, who was being carried back to bed after an evening stroll, when the moon had risen and it was already night.

PART III

HINDU STATES AND THEIR RULERS

CHAPTER XIV

A MODEL STATE

"Mysore is one of the best administered and most progressive of Indian States."

SIR WILLIAM P. BARTON, *late Resident of Mysore.*

"Sir Mirza Ismail appealed to the people of Mysore State to do everything that is possible to make it a worthy unit of the Federation of the future."

Address of the DEWAN *to the Mysore Representative Assembly, October,* 1934.

"A faint memory of the religious habit often haunts the throne."

"With justice I rule Mysore."

Sanskrit motto of the State.

TIPPU dead and the Muslim power entirely broken, the British Government at once restored the State to the Hindu family of Wadiyar in the person of their representative, a child of five, who was installed in the ivory chair, the "Lion Throne" of his ancestors, that is the sacred, cherished emblem of their sovereignty. It had to be rescued from an outhouse of Tippu's palace, where it had been carelessly pushed in and broken, and was repaired with haste for the ceremony that took place early in June.

Originally built of figwood overlaid with ivory, the beautiful creamy-white surface is now covered with gold and silver figures: the lion and swan, elephants, horses, chariots, gods and *devadasis*. From its handles depend tassels of pearls. Overhead is the pearl-fringed umbrella, emblem of royalty; and hovering above it, the mythical jewelled bird that never touches the ground. "The head on which its shadow falls will wear a crown."

A Sanskrit inscription is written around the umbrella: ninety-six lines of invocations, blessings and allusions to the moon, for the Wadiyar family claim descent from the Lunar race of kings. They are Rajputs and sons of the Moon God. "Afraid of defeat by the spotless moon of your fame, the moon serves you in the guise of an umbrella," say the Sanskrit verses.

The rule of the young Raja, who was installed by the British Commander-in-Chief in 1799, was not a success. He was a weakling in every sense of the word and wasteful. An era of misgovernment culminated in a popular rising, and in 1831 it was found necessary to put the administration under control of the Mysore Commission, picked British officers who restored order and financial stability.

This was a temporary measure. Rendition of the State to the Wadiyars took place fifty years later and when I came to Bangalore in 1894 the Maharaja had just died, suddenly, of poisoning from a septic tooth. He was absent from Mysore and no caste dentist was available. It was impossible for him to suffer pollution from contact with a Christian, or a Japanese, however expert. Moreover, since his last birthday, various omens had made him aware of his approaching death and he quietly accepted the decree of the stars and the gods. The Maharani was at once appointed Regent, during the minority of her son, whom I well remember as a boy of eleven, under the tutelage of Sir Stuart Fraser.

Now I have returned to find His Highness the experienced, honoured and beloved ruler of six millions, whose welfare has been promoted to an extent that is truly wonderful. It is said of him that he is a good judge of men: that he has the flair for appointing able supporters of the policy in force in this State for the benefit of the people.

In Mysore, the agriculturists, who are the backbone of the country, are represented by their own class in the legislative council, with an elected majority, and the executive government is in the hands of officials. This system has worked admirably and may be judged by obvious results. When malcontents tried to upset it recently and demanded "democratic reforms," the Dewan, Sir Mirza Ismail, "expressed surprise that such demands should be brought forward at a time like the present, when parliamentary democracy was decaying everywhere."

Assuredly, a ministry formed from the town-bred intelligentsia would not favour the peasant class and "the right of the Brahmins to control in the villages is absolute: their birth is evidence of superiority."[1] Everywhere in India, caste is in the air, and our own Labour Party in England are naught but *coolies* and are so designated by high-caste Hindus. They marvelled that a socialist régime was permitted to exist, although Manu had said, "In the fourth age outcaste kings will rule over the earth." "Caste is . . . the most rigorous system of class distinctions that the world has ever seen, inspired and justified by the doctrines of transmigration of the soul and *kharma.*"[2] It is "the essential part of every Hindu's make-up—all essential in this life and those to come."[3] "The essence of Hindu religion as to man's destiny excludes levelling."[4] The peasant is under the heel of the twice-born.

Not so in Mysore. "The record and progress of your State, since my last visit, eleven years ago, is certainly remarkable," said H.E. the Viceroy, when he passed through again in 1934. The fame of it has gone abroad. Future rulers come with their tutors to Bangalore, where are the Offices of the Administration, to study the art of government and learn the way in which they themselves should walk with wisdom.

The conditions of life for the people have improved beyond measure; not only in large towns, but in urban districts and the countryside. The *ryots* receive help and encouragement to improve the value of their crops and are grateful and responsive. The vegetables and

[1] *Behind Mud Walls*, C. and W. H. Wiser.

[2] *The Village Gods of South India*, Rt. Rev. H. Whitehead, D.D.

[3] *The Underworld of India*, Lieut.-Gen. Sir George McMunn, K.C.B., K.C.S.I., D.S.O.

[4] The *Morning Post*, June 17, 1935.

fruit of the Mysore and Bangalore markets can vie with the produce of Great Britain. At annual prize-givings (I have just been to one in the market of Mysore) old weather-beaten peasant women, as well as men, carry off little bags in which *rupees* do jingle. They have won them in competition for their plantains, their tomatoes, their brinjals, their marrows, their cucumbers. When a girl, how I grumbled at the food that came to our table in Bangalore. Though the cooking of it was excellent, everything—no matter what it was—tasted alike, or had no taste at all, except of condiments! I do not say that now.

It is ordered, industrial progress and the exploitation of natural resources that has effected this betterment: it is a deep personal interest of those at the head of affairs.

Not the least interesting exhibit hanging on the wall at the recent Industrial Fair of Dasara was a large map of Mysore, covered with tiny flags and not a square inch between, that showed how thoroughly the land had been tapped everywhere, by experts, to discover its resources. Thus I learned that ten thousand tons of granite are exported annually to Great Britain, and in this rich soil is to be found gold, silver, iron, lead, antimony, asbestos, chromite, clay, manganese, copper and other minerals. Iron, too, that is smelted by means of charcoal from the forest areas of Shimoga and Kadur.

Mines and Works are organized by Government and other activities were in evidence at the Dasara Exhibition, where different Departments had each a stall: Agriculture, Dairy Produce, Sericulture, Technical Trades and Toy-making, Health and Infant Welfare were all represented. There was soap from the Factory at Bangalore, and porcelain; household furniture of cane, or wood, elaborately carved or inlaid from the Mysore Technical Training Institute; electrical bulbs and fittings; the new sugar industry, boiled down to confectionery and sweets, as well as by-products; silks, georgettes and other fine fabrics from the Government silk mills. There is an Institute for training the Blind, Deaf and Dumb in spinning and weaving.

An aged blind woman was squatting on the floor spinning for *khaddar*, after the fashion that would gladden Mr. Gandhi's heart; but, unluckily, a man alongside was giving a demonstration of a hand-machine for the purpose, recently invented by a Madrassee, of which he turned the handle with astonishing rapidity and left the old system yards and yards behind.

In the Art Section were to be found in oils, or water-colours, pictures of gods and *gurus*, landscapes, posters and portraits of Tagore, the poet and the *Mahatma*, both well in the Public Eye at present. A more interesting one of Gandhi had been wrought with a needle and silks, so fine as to produce the illusion of the brush. I could hardly refrain from asking the young man who had achieved this masterpiece why he had not sought a more beautiful subject for his art and undoubted skill.

The Medical College was showing a variety of age-old Indian remedies for the ills of India—such as snake-bite—which they are trying to utilize with the help of western knowledge. In this connection it was interesting to read the experience of an expert on this poison. Few snakes, he says, inoculate with danger to life, excepting the cobra and Russell's viper. It is shock and fear that kill the victim, more often than not, and a cure is effected by a sublime faith in some medicament in use for many centuries, rather than by any antitoxin properties it may possess.

Sandalwood oil is a Government monopoly which brings in twenty *lakhs* of *rupees* yearly in export for medicine, perfume and soap, added to home consumption which must be immense, as it seems to outrival all other scents in favour, even attar of roses.

I have had the good fortune to see the various processes through which this costly wood must pass in the Government Factory of Mysore City, but the temperature necessary for distillation, together with the overpowering perfume, defeated me and made my visit shorter than I had wished.

A certain soil and a certain altitude are requisite for

the growth of this famous tree, and thirty to forty years must pass before it is of commercial value. Wood blocks are exported, in rough sacks, at the price of two thousand *rupees* per ton. Cut up into short logs, these are shaved by machinery, then hammered into pulp and ground into powder. There follows condensation by steam and a minutely careful chemical analysis before the oil is poured into aluminium bottles and sealed, ready for its long journey to Europe, especially to France.

From the Sandalwood Factory my kind guide motored me farther afield to the Welfare centre for babies; the infants of the very poor, from homes where the income ranges from ten to twelve *rupees* [1] per month. The mother brings her child twice in the day: in the morning for an oil or a water-bath and a bottle of good milk, and again in the late afternoon to be fed. Nurses are in attendance under a matron, and a doctor gives expert advice when necessary. Tubercular children are given sun-bath treatment, properly regulated to suit the need of each individual case.

There is no doubt the public conscience has been awakened in Mysore, for attention is now given to clearing out slums that are not seen unless sought for. To all appearance, it is a city so beautifully clean and well kept that no one could fail to remark upon it; nor is this merely by contrast with eastern towns of ill-repute; never a vestige of litter, nor any little heap of dirt! All done by invisible means, so that each morning, when my day began, I looked out over a Mysore that had been completely swept and garnished afresh: marvellously modern in the gleaming sunshine. I saw a city of big public offices, colleges, hospitals, sanatoria, institutions, perhaps a little like exhibition buildings, facing each other across well-laid motor roads: a market with food displayed to the best advantage and careful window-dressing, where flies are not. Even the mosquito scourge of South India is kept at bay.

Social duties and pleasures took me into a region of

[1] From 15*s*. to 18*s*. 6*d*.

parks and gardens and smooth roads intersected by large grass-planted circles, with high standards for electric lighting, that shed rays to all four points of the compass. Large, hospitably-open gates led to princely mansions: of the Yuveraj, when he comes to Mysore; of the Ranis and different Princesses of the Royal House; of the State guest-house where European visitors are entertained, till the farthest limit was reached and the car turned to face the splendid Fort Palace of the Maharaja, with its two wide gateways and temple, that stands out magnificently and is the very centre of the city and its heart.

Though the pulse of the city beat there, the Cosmic Force, the Divine Afflatus for the Hindu mind, flows down from the height Chamundi, an isolated peak of massive rock, a *droog* that forms a ridge-like background on the south-east side. There dwells in her temple the Goddess, the Eternal Feminine, who, in Mysore, is called Chamundeswari, titular deity of the royal family of Wadiyar.

Her High Priest is of secondary importance only to the Maharaja. When he goes abroad, his cortège is imposing; a bodyguard of cavalry escorts him, a camel, a sacred horse. I saw him borne shoulder-high in his luxurious litter (on his way to one of the palaces, where he spent some hours), half-reclining on cushions in gorgeous silken robes of apricot, that the sun blazed into flamingo shades; a gold crown upon his head.

A mere pilgrim to the shrine of the goddess will find the ascent of the thousand steps in a road branching off from the south-west corner of the race-course. Fortunately, for those who are aged, or infirm, it suffices for holiness to mount only a portion of the rugged stone stairway, as far as the small, black figure of Ganesh. Here may be seen most clearly the impress of two little feet, firmly outlined in the stone, where the goddess herself had rested, in far-away days beyond recalling, and had stayed awhile to exchange courtesies with her neighbour or, perchance, ask advice of the wisest of gods.

As Siva's spouse, Kali, or Durga-devi, she had been engaged in mortal combat with Bandasura, the embodiment in buffalo form of physical desires, and there were other demons of a like nature with whom she must contend. Mysore was in the grip of two of these, Chandi and Mandi, whom she engaged in a nine days' conflict, and on the tenth she was victorious. Then it was that she adopted the names of her conquered foes, in combination, became another aspect of Kali, and is called Sri Chamundeswari.

The goddess is two feet high and black (a priest of the temple told me), and she has ten arms that signify her great beneficence; an all-embracing motherhood. From time immemorial, Rajputs and Mahrattis have held a festival in honour of her victory, the "Ten Days," the Dasara, that is coincident with Navarati, more universally observed by Hindus all over India, but for a day less, as its name denotes.

They are festivals of the autumn equinox, at a turn of the wheel of the year, when the change in nature affects men also: some are in need of diversion, but pious souls spend their days in fasting and prayer. Dasara is unique and has its marked social side, which has been observed in Mysore since 1654 with Oriental splendour, and the procession of the Tenth Day—the Day of Victory—is unsurpassed in Southern India.

For nine days previously, the Maharaja "is regarded as becoming for the time, the representative of the Goddess Chamundi and the intermediary for the conveyance of her blessing to her people." In those nine days she takes on different aspects. For the first three she is Siva's spouse, the Kali engaged in conflict with desire: the goddess, who guards her children of Mysore from misfortune and disease. During the next three days she is Lakshmi, bride of Vishnu, goddess of wealth and prosperity. "The crops are ripening, pour out thy blessing upon us." For the last three days she is Saraswati, wife of Brahma, the Creator, source of enlightenment, patroness of Learning and the Arts. It is an auspicious time for a lad to begin his education. "May Saraswati give me intellect and the Sun give me light!"

The Maharaja, a most pious Hindu, fasts during the nine days, is unshaven and worships an image of the family goddess in the private oratory of the Palace. For he never leaves the precincts until the tenth day, when he goes forth in royal state to celebrate her victory, mounted on the sacred elephant, in a howdah of silver and gold, with the Yuveraj, his brother, beside him and the young heir seated behind.

There are preludes to the great occasion, as every day of Dasara has its own function. The ceremonies open on the first day, when the ruler of Mysore enters the Durbar Hall of thirty pillars and simultaneously a member of the Royal Family carries in the State Sword, the symbol of power. The Maharaja seats himself on a low stool for half an hour during *puja* by the attendant priests. He then walks to the throne in his jewelled sandals, pays reverence to it, where has been placed and removed before his arrival, the image of a lion; passes round it three times and at last mounts from the seven steps on the right side to the *simhasana*.[1] He takes the salute; the palace band plays the National Anthem of Mysore; the *purohits*, chanting Vedic hymns, sprinkle him with holy water and bless him; whilst Brahmins bring offerings of coconut and sacred rice, and courtiers make obeisance before the throne, overlaid with cloth of gold and satin cushions, to the gorgeously clad, impassive figure seated there.

It is on the seventh day that Saraswati comes into her own and that the palace books and manuscripts are collected together for special worship. Instruments of labour are venerated, that they may work well and bring good fortune to the owner, who censes his tools, and on the ninth morning of Dasara I went to the "*Puja* of Animals" who are brought before His Highness at the Palace that he and the priest may bless them. A *pandal*, a pavilion built above the ground level, had been erected in the grounds just outside the back of the Palace for the

[1] *Simha*, lion; *asana*, seat.

Maharaja, his brother, and the Brahmins. There came to a standstill, momentarily, one animal after another, most splendidly caparisoned, all conscious of their importance and dignity. First, the sacred State Elephant, who saluted with a shower of red rose petals flung upward from his trunk; the sacred white horse, the "dancing" pony, sacred cows decorated with draperies and garlanded with flowers, their horns coloured gold. All were blessed in turn and I could see the smoke of incense burning before each one passed, to be followed by all manner of vehicles; silver palanquins, chariots, coaches, carriages, the State litter of Tippu Sultaun and the most modern of motor-cars decked with flowers as for a carnival on the Riviera.

On Victory Day the morning ceremony was concerned with the worship of the Royal arms and State sword, which were subsequently piled in palanquins and sent off to the Parade Ground three miles outside the city, there to await the coming of the Maharaja and troops in the late afternoon.

By four o'clock the whole population of Mysore had found place somewhere and somehow along the line of route northward from the Palace to the Banni-Mandap. From a covered stand erected outside the Gates for the guests of his Highness, the procession could be seen and enjoyed to the full; its colour, its symbolism, its variety; its eastern splendour and its significance to prince and people. Camels headed it; elephants with huge gold bosses tapering from forehead to trunk, anklets and draperies of gold tissue to the ground; horses, richly caparisoned, from the royal stables; infantry in red trousers and green tunics; cavalry in a dark blue uniform and striped *puggarees*, regimental bands, bodyguard, *sirdars* in a large closed vehicle drawn by an elephant; the white "dancing" pony; a baby elephant making its début alongside its mother and given refreshment at intervals of its long march; standard-bearers with twirled silk banners, discs, umbrellas, all emblems of state; the great antediluvian animal, the sacred elephant, with its burden of royalty encased in a gold howdah; a wondrous spectacle.

When all had gone by, holders of car passes hastened to the Parade Ground to take up a good position for the review, drink tea and while away the time till the procession should appear, slowly climbing the long hill to the Banni-Mandap.

This name is taken from a splendid tree that once grew there and is sacred, for on such another the five Pandava brothers had occasion to hide their arms, with which they subsequently won a victory. Also this "tree of energy" [1] was used from time immemorial to generate by friction the divine spark of fire for the sacrifice of Dasara. It is gone! but a bough is placed in the *Mandapam*, where the Maharaja alights for a rest, that he may there perform the worship of past days and prick the bark. May it bleed! If the sap be of a reddish tint it is an omen of good fortune for a twelvemonth, a year of victory.

The afternoon wore on to its close and when His Highness descended from the howdah, red clouds about the setting sun had lost their brilliance. So the light faded while he broke his ten days' fast, was shaved, was given the ceremonial bath.

Meanwhile the Parade Ground had been cleared by the police, the troops marched in and took up their positions; officers and men waited silently in the gloom of lengthening shadows.

Night fell and all the land was dark!

Suddenly, dramatically, the field was lighted from end to end. A brilliant, dazzling illumination lit up the scene.

Royally clad, splendidly mounted on a black charger, a perfect seat, the Maharaja surrounded by his staff rode on to the field, a dream vision of ancient, princely Rajput romance.

[1] *Prossopis picegera.*

CHAPTER XV

INDIAN NIGHTS' ENTERTAINMENT

"Moreover the King made a great throne of ivory, and overlaid it with pure gold.

And there were six steps to the throne, with a footstool of gold, which were fastened to the throne."

2 Chron. ix. 17, 18.

When the Victory Review is over with the march past and the salute, the Vijayadasami procession forms up again, to wend its way back slowly to the city, escorted by a troop of bearers, whose flambeaux in these days, are fitted with dazzling, acetylene lamps. The Palace is reached at midnight and the closing of the Gates signals the finish of entertainments of the past ten Indian nights.

Every evening of Dasara that preceded its apotheosis, the Maharaja had held a Durbar: eight levées for his Indian subjects and one to which were also invited European officials and guests. This has been the custom of Mysore since 1805.

The Hall where these functions are held may best be described as similar to the auditorium of an opera house, but not semi-circular in shape. There is one long, straight stretch of grand balcony that overhangs a vast courtyard, set ready with a temporary stage for wrestlers that is easily removable. On it, and all round about within the open court, are enacted a succession of eastern variety shows, some to the music of the palace bands, some without, whilst carnival figures and men on stilts make their appearance at times to lend an added picturesqueness to the scene. The illuminations are almost comparable to, if not so magical, as Eastern sunshine.

The chairs of the guests in the balcony are on

graduated levels, facing the Ivory Throne, with its pearl-fringed umbrella, set on the highest tier in the centre of this long, unusual balcony-hall. It has a gallery running along the whole length at the back, gauze-curtained, for the royal ladies and those of the household, who are *gosha*, to peer through slits at their lords seated below them and the distant spectacle. Those less élite, but more fortunate in unveiled freedom, occupy two tiers of opera boxes at both ends and fill them to advantage with a blaze of gorgeous coloured *saris*.

One night of an Indian Durbar, I sat in a box that had been reserved for European spectators, looking straight out from it to the throne, behind which were grouped the temple *pujaris*, Brahmins all, for though "every Brahmin is not a priest, every priest must be a Brahmin." What a wealth of exquisite colouring was there in the soft Kashmiri shawls and turbans. About seventy of them—perhaps more—were robed in shades of apricot, of reds, of crimsons, and the curious, brilliant blue-green that is a sacred colour and they made a superb background for the ivory and gold chair and the silk-clad figure, that moved ever so slightly, from time to time, as his courtiers bowed in long lines to the right, or the left of him.

That night there were no chairs. Hundreds of men, white trousered and long coated in black alpaca, with gold-edged turbans and some with gold sashes, covered all the steps and crouched on the red-carpeted floor.

In order of precedence, ten or twelve were marshalled in one long line, on one side, and the other alternately and as they bowed low from the waist with oriental suppleness and grace, the *udaspadavis* chanted in lovely harmonies: "Krishnaraja Maharaja, your officers make their obeisance, be so gracious as to look this way." The gold-turbaned head turned to the right, or left, and the two upright hands, palms pressed closely and to the finger-tips, gave welcome, till all had been presented to their spiritual lord and prince.

Peons hastened to decorate the guests with garlands

of jasmine blossoms: bands in the courtyard below played the National Anthem of Mysore: the company of athletes awaiting each their turn to strip and wrestle—a very fine performance of its kind—had sent two pairs of men onto the stage.

Simultaneously horses, with men in the saddle, both trained to think and act as one being, gave a musical ride. When it was over, the stage was opened down its whole centre to make a passage way for the State Elephant, painted with a conventional device of leaves, decorated with a gold boss and anklet, draped magnificently, that he might salute the Maharaja and the Court by a toss of his trunk and a shower of rose petals.

The pageant was over for the night.

* * * * *

The European Durbar is held on the ninth and last night of Dasara and I drove through the gates of a Palace of Enchantment, for the splendid building was outlined and ablaze with thousands of lights.

Within the entrance, an exotic atmosphere, scent of sandalwood, perfume of Venus, filled the hot air as I slowly ascended the wide marble staircases. The Indian ladies' gallery and the opera boxes were already crowded, when I reached the Durbar Hall and took up my position in the crowd of assembled guests: men in conventional evening garb, or uniform and decorations; women in gay shoulder straps and long skirts of lovely hues.

As far as possible in order of precedence, we moved along behind the Ivory Chair and then at the end of the Hall, where I turned, I found myself alone. My name was passed on from one secretary to another, to be announced when I reached the throne.

I stood before it, facing the impassive Maharaja, to whom I bowed and passed on to my seat for the entertainment to follow. When all was over and this ceremony repeated, His Highness bent forward and gave me a bouquet sprayed with sandalwood and attar of roses.

All the men present had garlands thrown round their necks by the *peons* and when leaving the palace, every woman held a perfumed bouquet in her hands. At intervals of the long processions of guests the *udaspadavis* murmured their soft chant, "Krishnaraja Maharaja, salaam!"

On these occasions, the British Resident comes in state, in a lovely barouche drawn by four horses and with outriders; the imposing, dignified fashion of a past age. He takes his seat on a gold chair to the right of His Highness, whose brother, the Yuveraj, occupies another on his left side.

All were seated. The wrestlers made ready for the trial of skill on the platform and again the arena at the back was the scene of a musical ride; but afterwards, instead of "our lord the elephant," dancers appeared, waving vivid red- or gold-coloured silk handkerchiefs. There were eighteen of them in one long line across the courtyard and they gave us a folk dance that was reminiscent of Southern Spain. Amidst this social splendour, it served to recall the other aspect of the Dasara. "The crops are ripening; pour out thy blessing, oh, Lakshmi, goddess of wealth and prosperity, *shakti* of Vishnu! We dance, to the forthcoming harvest."

As in Europe, so also in India, is a revived interest in folk dancing and the Panjur Sholagas had been bidden to Mysore City from the Biligirrirangan Hills to perform at the Industrial Exhibition. I saw them one night, a group of half naked hill people, give a realistic jungle hunt of some wild beast of their forests. After a tremendous *tom-toming*, which needed lighted fires to keep their drum-skins taut, they started off with wild leaps on their expedition. Then their movements became slower, quiet, more stealthy, till they closed up round their prey and finished with a kill.

Another evening was set apart for a professor of *yogi* and also his pupils to give us demonstrations of deep breathing, that is essential for perfect control of muscles and limbs and even of life under abnormal conditions and to effect union with the Divine Spirit. At Hoshangabad during this Dasara, a disciple of the art had allowed himself to be buried up to his chest in earth, that was sown with wheat. For the nine days of the festival he remained thus in a deep trance, apparently lifeless, and the plants were a foot high when he came back again to consciousness. Where had he been meanwhile?

Nothing so sensational as this happened for me to see, but the professor had one show pupil, who most surely will become an adept. I see him, a few years hence, seated under a banyan tree, on the skin of a spotted deer, his matted hair coiled on the top of his head, one thin leg stretched straight out in front of him, the other curled comfortably round his neck: a begging bowl at hand for alms from the pious Hindus.

In short, from the 9th of October until the end of the month, Mysore kept high holiday. There was cricket, volley ball, tennis, billiards and bridge, military sports and public flights by the Madras Flying Club from the race-course in the day time. At night there were cinema shows and religious plays in Tamil at the Raja Lakshmi Theatre facing the Clock Tower, that is a landmark in the town.

The play that I saw was a modern variant of the deeds of Krishna, the Hindu Hercules, who attained divinity as the eighth *avatar* of Vishnu. He is much honoured in Mysore and on the façade of the Technical Institute may be seen a life-size, blue baby figure of the hero of the Mahabhrata, whose death heralded the *Kali yuga*, our present, unlucky world-age. Hindu fancy has been caught and held especially by his adventures with milkmaids, before he was aware of his divinity, but these episodes were robbed of all offence in "Sri Krishna-Leela" by representing its hero as a mischievous, teasing, naughty boy, an *enfant terrible*. The part was admirably played by a little girl, daughter of the manager of the theatre, an artist to her finger tips, and it is sad to think that one so gifted must soon relinquish her profession, as women's parts are invariably taken by lads. It was difficult to realize that the milkmaids were really youths, whose own, long hair coiled and twisted and bedecked with flowers completed all other suggestions of femininity.

The production was interesting; something of a pantomime with Transformation scenes; something of a mystery with the advent of Brahmin priests on the stage: the costumes colourful and harmonious. However, as the play began only at 10 p.m. and was not quite finished at two o'clock in the morning, I have not felt disposed to go again to the theatre for study of the Hindu Scriptures.

Yet I spent one superb, tropical night at the *puja* of Sri Chamundeshwari, whose temple stands on the hill overlooking Mysore, at the end of the long ridge that has been so successfully lighted by apparent archways on the winding, motor road; that is an easier way for the pilgrim to the top, than the thousand steps on the other side.

The moon was at the full and hung, solitary, in the heavens, a huge, round, silver disc. Though there were no stars to rival the innumerable Temple lamps, many coloured globes outlined the lake that lies, almost hidden away, in a deep hollow at the foot of the prominence and there was no darkness visible. The huge, carved pyramid of the temple could be seen outlined against a sombre background of sky. Time and again, a sudden gleam, a shaft of summer lightning, seemed to herald the exit of Chamundeshwari in processional guise of silk and jewels and garlands: her coming to the water's edge, where the high-caste ladies watched the proceedings from a *pandal*; her entrance into the gold shrine, fitted up in a swanboat, that had been immovable, awaiting her beside the shore. A salute for her—or was it for His Highness, the Maharaja, who had come from the Palace to be present at the festival in honour of the goddess of her family?

The swans, a pair of them, both fore and aft, impelled by some unseen force, made the circuit of the still lagoon and as they floated into their first haven, the car turned past the corner of a rock and we were speeding back to the town before the rush of general departure.

Far below, covering all the plain, illuminated at every point, as if the great idea was to outshine the light of day, lay Mysore: a brilliant, farewell vision to linger in one's memory of the City of Beautiful Night.

CHAPTER XVI

TRAVELS IN THE "LAND OF THE CELESTIALS" [1]

"Since I have been in India I have had a great desire to visit the State of Travancore.

Here Nature has spent upon the land her richest bounties: the sun fails not by day, the rain falls in due season, drought is practically unknown and an eternal sunshine gilds the scene. Where the land is capable of culture there is no denser population; where it is occupied by jungle, or backwater, or lagoon, there is no more fairy landscape."

LORD CURZON, *Viceroy of India.*

THE brilliance of the preceding night had shamed the dawn of the morrow and the sun had hidden himself behind a bank of cloud, when I started on my journey out of Mysore State, which is bounded on every side by British India.

As sometimes happens in life, I had choice of two ways into Travancore. Having heard much of the beauty of the water-ways from Cochin to Trivandrum, the capital, I chose the longer, more difficult route and determined to travel by slow and easy stages to the wonderland of the south-west coast and subsequently to the Land's End of India, Cape Comorin.

The few miles of railway to Nanjungud was not worth consideration and the motor road was reported to be in fairly good condition, despite the recent *monsoon*, which had necessitated repairs at intervals. The sun put in his appearance with midday force and it was soon pleasurable to gain the shelter of the beautiful woods that edge the Game Preserve of Mysore State, close to the frontier, where a high archway marks the line of demarcation.

[1] Venad (*Travancore*).

It was after a picnic lunch by the wayside that progress became the slower as the road grew steep, and I found myself on my way to revisit the Hill Stations of British India, that I had not thought to see again. Nor did they give me as cheery a welcome as during my longer stay in April, under a summer sky. This was late October and I could better understand the much-vaunted resemblance of Ooty to the Homeland, for which I now acknowledge there is much to be said. A heavy mist concealed hill-tops, now and then to descend in gentle rain; the green, fresh beauty of the trees, the soft air and the lovely light of English autumnal evenings were indeed reminiscent, especially of the countryside where pines and silver birches grow.

At my next stage, Coonoor, nearly two thousand feet lower, the illusion was lost in dense, tropical growth, and the climate was less chilly and bone searching, for the temperature, at its coldest, is never below sixty degrees.

Seventeen miles down the hill, at the junction of railways, I came once more to the beautiful areca nut and plantain grove that held my fancy, and this time was a herald, though I did not know it, of the marvellous tropical scenery of Cochin and Travancore.

Legends assert oft and again that the entrance to wonderland is none too easy and that it may even be preceded by nightmare, which hedges in the celestial kingdom of our dreams. I confess, that from the time of my arrival on the outskirts, at Podanur, I began to consider seriously whether this journey, that was so disagreeable, might in the end prove worth while. What would wonderland give me in return?

After a night spent in the only accommodation available, a bedroom at the Junction itself, where all the noises of railway traffic and shunting and diabolical whistles made sleep impossible, I took the first train to Cochin. There I had hoped to see something of the Sons of Israel, the communities of Black and White Jews, numbering about three hundred, and a synagogue famous for its flooring of ancient Chinese tiles, relics of an early trade. The wonderful scientific fishing nets the Chinamen introduced I did see and the impress they left on the physiognomy of the people, and even on the picturesque Dutch houses which have such a curious twirl at either end of their gabled roofs, not reminiscent of Holland, but of Chinatown.

Ages ago, Phœnicians had come to the Malabar coast and traders from Palestine in the days of King Solomon, who wanted gold and silver, ivory, apes and peacocks: also from Arabia and Persia to barter their wares in exchange for sandalwood, the "bird with the tail", and spices, more especially pepper.

In the middle centuries, the Portuguese sent a "Viceroy of India" in the person of one of their adventurous seamen, Almeyda. In 1515, yet another, Albuquerque, who established headquarters for his country at Goa and obtained almost a monopoly of the trade in spices between Cochin and Quilon. The latter place had a queen of its own in those days and only later was incorporated in Travancore State.

Then came the Dutch, who defeated the Portuguese and last of all the peaceful penetration of the British East India Company that absorbed the trade and drove away competitors.

It was disappointing to find that there was no place in Cochin, where I could lodge and that the Travellers' Bungalow, two miles away at Ernakulam, the terminus of the State Railway, was pronounced "impossible," "unfit for habitation."

A Travellers' Bungalow, or "T.B.," as it is familiarly called, is an institution of South India, without which there could be no travelling, unless with tents. One, at least, is to be found at a place of any importance, mainly for the use of officials passing through from one district to another. They have a prior claim to such rooms as it may contain, generally two or three suites of bed and bathrooms and a common dining-room, but bona fide travellers may stay for a period of three days, or even more, if no other applicants arrive asking hospitality. The fees are low and there are, usually, a butler and cook who provide meals, but no one in India travels without a servant, if only for the sake of prestige. In the large towns there are hotels and occasionally the comfortable British Clubs have married quarters and welcome strangers who have introductions.

Quite evidently, Cochin has not been predisposed towards an influx of tourists, but the day has come when hustle and travellers can no longer be evaded. Her harbour facilities have been immensely improved of late and I saw a big liner sailing in gaily, that would have been barred out by a too narrow access all these past years. Cochin State, Travancore and British India have combined in this recent enterprise; the railway line has been altered to broad guage to meet the anticipated increase of trade and traffic and it is said that an hotel for Europeans is actually in course of construction.

This fact, however interesting, was not helpful to me, who could not find a place to lay my head, and in such a dilemma there seemed no alternative but to at once take the boat and sail along the beautiful backwaters, as I had planned to do, but not in such hot haste. My romanticist friends had said that I must wait for a night of full moon to see the fairyland to its best advantage, but the silver lamp was untrimmed and the heavens unusually dark. Moreover, rain threatened. It was possible to hire a private motor launch, but where, and from whom I had not the remotest idea. Nor had anyone else whom I questioned. As the South Indian Railway has no connection with the steamers that ply to and fro Ernakulam and Quilon, the station-master's mind was a complete blank on the subject; and his subordinates had too many opinions, all diverse and all equally unreliable. I sent my bearer into Cochin by rickshaw to make the best arrangement he could and when I arrived at the departure stage myself at 11.30 p.m. and saw the boat in which I was to enjoy an exquisite night of marvellous scenery, my stout heart nearly failed me. Only the camp cot specially provided under cover made the journey possible and I resigned myself to the awful inevitability of fate till morning dawned.

By half-past eight o'clock we were well out of Cochin State and had arrived at Alleppey, a roadstead with a unique, natural breakwater of heavy oil and mud deposited on the seabed in a semi-circle, which has served to make this town the second largest in Travancore State. The mud bank ensures six miles of smooth water along the coast where is an incalculable wealth of natural produce easily available; such as coconut cake and oil, coir fibre, matting and rope; cachou nuts, ginger and other spices, arrowroot, tea and fish.

All passengers disembarked here and no matter what wonders I might miss on the water-ways, sailing over canals, rivers and lakes; or what interesting glimpses of the native life on the shores, I firmly refused to be transhipped into a still smaller steamer to Quilon. The Maharaja's highway was good enough for me and very beautiful I found it under the shade of waving coconut palms, thousands upon thousands of trees and stretches of paddy fields worked by the lowest caste, the Pulayas, who have a folk lore and songs all their own of the countryside "with their burden of love and labour and the beauty of earth."

It was enchanting to find myself "where dwelleth the goddess of prosperity,"[1] my kind friend Lakshmi again to my rescue from the minor disagreeables of tourism.

Nor did she fail me, but directed my next travels in comfort and into pleasant places and under her guidance I saw the more remote beauties of the country of her choice; one of the loveliest it has been my good fortune to visit.

No wonder Tippu Sultaun dreamed of its conquest after his invasion of Malabar in 1789, when Cochin became a tributary State. He made similar and impossible demands of the Raja of Travancore, with which

[1] *Travancore*, i.e. Sri-Vazhum-Kodu.

that ruler refused to comply and soon found himself at war with the Muslims.

Hitherto the Western Ghats, covered by primæval forest and dense jungle, had intimidated would-be invaders, and the mountain passes, little used now, were dangerous. Its natural fortifications had been the great protection of the State hitherto, but Tippu swept through Malabar, winning one battle after another and penetrated as far as Alwaye, in Travancore. Then Nature intervened in the most unexpected way. The *monsoon* broke stormily, and before due date, lashing the great River Periyar into flood and fury, drenching the Muslims and their ammunition. Moreover, Tippu the Tiger had maintained his reputation for ferocity by slaying the inhabitants and also burning their homes, so that the track of his army was a desert waste, without shelter for his men in their retreat. It was the retribution of Ganesh, said the Hindus, for Tippu's hideous brutalities to female elephants! The Raja of that period presented seven gold ones to the temple of Ettamanur, in commemoration of his victory, which was rendered decisive for ever by the British attack on the Sultaun's eastern territory, to which he was forced to give all his time and attention, till his defeat and death at Seringapatam. The English saved Malabar, where Tippu had destroyed the pepper vines and coconut trees to keep away the European traders.

Not only Hindu Temples had been polluted by the fanatical Muslims, but they desecrated Christian Churches also. Christianity had been established in South Cochin since A.D. 52, when tradition says St. Thomas landed on an island of the lagoon near Cranganore. He afterwards proceeded to Madras, where he was martyred by the Brahmins and St. Thomas's Mount with its Cathedral, built over the remains of the Apostle, has become a place of pilgrimage for Roman Catholics.

In the eighth century, another Thomas appeared on the scene. He was an Armenian, who had two wives and an enormous family, amongst whom his property was divided up at his death. His children combined with the rest of the Christian community at Cranganore and they all came to look upon *Mar*[1] Thomas as their common ancestor. Yet a third tradition says that Thomas of Cana brought four hundred colonists from Mesopotamia to Cranganore earlier than the eighth century and they obtained permission from the Raja to build shops and churches in a street opposite the palace. All the Christian foreigners settled on the south side and the native converts on the north, and this gave rise to the terms Sudhist and Nordist Christians, but the distinction is racial and they all call themselves Syrians, in the belief that, "their ancestors were converts from Judaism to the Syro-Chaldean rite of Christianity, by St. Thomas the Apostle, before they came to Malabar."

When the Portuguese rose to power in the sixteenth century in Cochin and Travancore, they found the Nestorian heresies were prevalent in all the churches and they determined to put an end to that. They established the Inquisition at Goa, their headquarters, and by every means possible, forced the unhappy Syrian Christians into the arms of Rome. Archbishop Menezes burnt their ancient liturgies and Syriac manuscripts and books and completely abolished Nestorianism aided by the civil and military authorities under the Portuguese Governor of Cochin. The Holy Office did the rest. The Syrian Christians submitted to their fate, and as a concession were permitted to use the Syriac language in their liturgy. Every church has three altars and they are said to resemble the Copts in their worship.

It was an unwilling submission for the most part. When the Protestant Dutch defeated the Portuguese about 1653, forty thousand armed Syrian Christians renounced their allegiance to Rome at Mantancheri in Cochin. They gathered round the Coonen Cross and as the word Coonen means "bent" it may be questioned if it were the *swastika*, or one of the early granite crosses

[1] Saint, Lord.

that stood in front of a Christian Church, possibly out of the perpendicular. "With a view to enabling a larger number to touch the cross, when abjuring allegiance, long ropes were tied to it and those who touched the ropes, had touched the cross."[1]

In the beginning of the nineteenth century the Church Missionary Society sent three of their missionaries to Kottayam, in Travancore, to work with the Syrian Christians and this union was wonderfully successful for over twenty years, during which the Bible was translated into Malayalam. It was rather too ideal to last and finally there was a split in the camp. Some Syrians then joined the Church of England and there are at the present time eight different denominations in Travancore, of which the Romo-Syrian community outnumbers the rest, and represents more than one-third of the whole population. The Rajas have always been extremely tolerant of an alien faith and this is the "Land of Charity and Piety." St. Mary's Jacobite church at Niranum near Thiruvella, one as old as Christianity itself in Travancore, is cheek by jowl with an equally ancient Hindu temple.

Entirely ignorant at the time of my journey of the religious vicissitudes of the State, I had been surprised to see so many churches by the roadside and under the shade of coconut palms, where they looked singularly out of place, and to hear their bells ringing for service. Though one recognized many Christian women amongst the passers-by from the heavy gold rings in their ears, the position of which they change when they marry, the men on the roads seemed chiefly Hindu. It happened to be early in December, the week of Ashtami, a very important festival at Vaikom, which is attended by thousands of pilgrims from all over India. The watermen who punted the car over the ferry were all wearing Siva's sign manual round their necks, a single *rudra* bead strung on wire. They said they were going to the temple, as soon as they could get away from their work.

[1] Rev. J. Stewart.

A TYPICAL BACKWATER SCENE ON THE WEST COAST

HILLMEN STRIKING A LIGHT

Hinduism had a revival in honour of Siva in the tenth century and many pagodas are dedicated to Mahadeo, the Great God.

I was then returning from a visit to the head of Lake Periyar, a perfectly ideal spot near the source of Travancore's largest river where I had been lodged in a most luxurious Camp. It was constructed entirely of etter, a species of junglewood, which is a godsend to the forest dwellers of the hill country all around Peermade. They use only one small hatchet for their building operations, with which they hack down the tree, using its trunk for the structure and stripping bare and shaping its branches for the framework of roof and walls. The squares thus formed are then stuffed with the leaves placed criss-cross over each other until the whole construction is both air and water-tight. Lastly, windows are made like sliding panels, shelves put up along the partitions of the rooms and doors that are tied by cord to some support. At the entrance was a lounge hall; across the passageway, a dining-room and to right and left suites of writing-rooms, bedrooms, dressing-rooms and bath-rooms. All of them were both large and lofty.

The hill men had taken two months for the completion of this unique shooting lodge; beautifully situated at the head of the lake with a wonderful view across its waters to shores covered with forest, where bison and elephants come down to drink at eventide. A most romantic spot, full of wild animal life and of the rich warm colours of trees that are indigenous, deeply rooted in the soil of their homeland.

It had been a long trek to get there, but every mile of the route from Trivandrum was full of beauty and most varied interest. The countryside has been planned for the benefit of its inhabitants, who have no need of money since everything necessary for the simple life is God-given. I felt that presently, I should come across the Swiss Family Robinson, whose experiences were recalled by the vegetation and its many uses for food and shelter and clothing: some of the hill people are clad in leaves.

All about Trivandrum is the rich, red alluvial soil where coconuts and plantains flourish. Their foliage is the most decorative of any in the world of trees and to see them in their thousands is quite unforgettable. Of the former it is said proverbially throughout Malabar, that no part of the coconut is without its use. Out of its wood the home is built and thatched with its leaves. Fibre from the husks provides mats for the dwelling and they are freed from dust by long strands stripped from the boughs. Brown sugar can be manufactured from the sap and the shells make the hottest charcoal obtainable for heating and cooking. The fruit itself is both food and drink. I know of none more delicious in a hot climate than coconut milk, germ free, cool, nutritious and refreshing, especially on a journey.

"The coconut bears heavy bunches and gives men its nectar-like water . . . in grateful remembrance of the water given to it in its younger days." In short, the words of the Muhammedam Malfuzat-i-Timuri seem to apply more especially to Travancore. "The whole country of India," said he, "is full of the plants that grow there and are fit for making wearing apparel and aromatic plants and sugar cane and the whole country is pleasant. For that reason it seems it should be ours." That idea still exists in India amongst the Muslims.

After some miles the landscape opened out with large patches of tapioca (one anna's worth of which will keep a man from starvation for a day), paddy fields and vegetable gardens about Kottayam.

This was the first stage of our journey; to spend a night in a Travellers' Bungalow, that is like the home of a well-off European; more comfortable and better furnished than any other of its kind that I have halted at elsewhere. There is a reason for this and the excellence of the servants in charge. Many distinguished people have come hitherward and rested on their way into and out of Travancore and it is practically a guest-house of the State. It was dark when we arrived but next morning had a lovely view for my delighted eyes, of paddy fields partially submerged and distant tree-clad hills.

All through the first day's journey we had travelled due north, but a few miles out of Kottayam, where the road approaches the Minachil River, it bends round eastward. Here were pepper gardens, and in the villages nearly every house door had mats spread out on the ground before it, covered with the year's harvest of pepper corns drying in the sunshine.

The land which had been gently undulating, now became more hilly and we arrived in the rubber country, which was to be our second stage at the bungalow of a planter, three miles within the gates of the estate. Fortunately it was well situated in a large clearing and garden, and had all the amenities of modern life; sanitation, electric light and gramophone, for rubber trees with their long, thin trunks are distinctly ugly and it must be terribly depressing to be on such a plantation when it rains. But the views over the jungle to distant hills and to Peermade, our next stage, is compensation in fine weather.

On the trek again meant climbing a short road up the *ghat*, where we came to the tea country, a plateau sixty miles long and twenty broad, that forms the boundary between Travancore and British India. There are over twenty thousand acres under cultivation and nearly as much in reserve, at first for coffee which was swept out by disease, and now for tea.

Peermade Hills were first discovered as a permanent residence by a Muslim saint, Pyr Muhammed, from whom they take their name, who lived and died there and a little white-washed *Koubba* stands out against the skyline, built over his remains. Now there is also a Residency, a church, club, tennis courts and golf links, for the altitude of 3,600 feet makes of it a pleasant Hill Station for Travancore. The Senior Maharani has just built a palace for herself and her family in a beautiful situation and intends occupying it next March during the hot weather of the Plains, which lasts three months. This is the fourth of Her Highness's princely homes and as she is fond of fine landscape and most artistic in her selection, they are all of them enviable to live in. She likes, more especially, to look from a height over a large expanse of water, river, lake, or sea and has found the sites she most desired at Peermade by the Periyar; overlooking Vellayani Lake at Trivandrum and a dream castle at Kovalam twelve miles distant from the town on a headland fronting the Arabian Sea. Her Highness has called it "Halcyon", and her charming personality is in keeping with its name.

My host, the Game Warden, has a bungalow at Peermade, but we were only lunching at it and pushed on to our destination in the afternoon. The motor launch met us at the lakeside and we embarked for tea and an ideal sail on the lake's smooth waters, when elephant and bison come down from jungle and hills to drink. Even a tigress, in charge of a small black panther, was much interested in the progress of the boat on another afternoon and sat watching it attentively until joined by her cub and the two of them moved on to their lair.

There is excellent shooting to be had all about these Hills and the tribesmen of the jungles, who live in trees well out of the reach of elephants, tigers, leopards, bison and wild boar, are splendid *shikaris*. Fishing in the Periyar River is as good as any in the world.

The mastery of this turbulent river has been one of the great feats of British engineers. Sixty years ago a large tract of land was leased near its source from the Maharaja for a thousand years. A dam and tunnel were constructed, and later, six miles of canal distribution that made a fertile land of the arid district around Madura. Thirty thousand cubic feet of water was made available for irrigation to the incalculable benefit of the people and the immense increase of wealth in Travancore State. Lake Periyar covers more than eight thousand acres and is a thing of beauty and a joy for ever.

Now that there is a movement afoot amongst civilized people for the preservation of wild life, no better site could have been found in Travancore for a National Park. It is to be hoped that small islands may be set apart as sanctuaries for breeding spotted deer and other beautiful creatures, that have been almost completely shot out by poachers from British India. It is a problem that a Provincial Government Assembly will face shortly at Simla. Unfortunately it will be "difficult to persuade 350,000,000 people that, at certain times of year or within certain areas, marauding tigers, bears, or panthers, the edible flesh of bird or beast, or marketable hide is better alive than dead and must be deliberately kept alive."

CHAPTER XVII

BIRTHDAY FESTIVITIES

"In this India never do the legitimate sons of great kings or princes or barons inherit the goods of their parents, but only the sons of their sisters."

Marumakkatayam Law of Malabar.

"Charity is our household divinity."

Sanskrit motto of Travancore.

THE 6th of November, the birthday of His Highness the Maharaja of Travancore, and I had just arrived at Trivandrum in time to witness the procession in the early morning.

A little party of us had seats in the long, narrow verandah of the old Durbar Hall, on an upper floor overlooking the principal street on the line of route. Whilst waiting we made a tour of inspection, taking a surreptitious look at the ivory throne, swathed in dust sheets. There were many old pictures of members of the Royal family, and engravings on the walls, and one of these especially attracted my notice. It was a Durbar of Mysore held by the Maharaja, who was enthroned after Tippu's death by General Harris. The hall in which it took place was burnt down, and another built of similar design, but still larger and more effective: the courtyard below is much the same as to-day, and Chamundi Hill, which changeth not, can be seen in the distance.

By this time the sacred elephants had mustered at the end of the street, and the riderless horses of the late Maharaja, that would never be mounted by anyone again: and boy scouts formed up in line on the other side of the road. But the auspicious moment for the Maharaja's departure had not been signalled, so we crossed the garden to the uninhabited, but fully furnished, palace

A NAYAR WOMAN

within the same enclosure as the Durbar Hall. It was two storeyed and decorated after the florid, French style of the early nineteenth century with pictures and ornaments obviously purchased during a Continental tour; Sèvres and Meissen china from France and Germany. The most interesting piece of furniture was an old-fashioned Indian swing cot; a long, straight plank hung on thick silver chains, where a former ruler liked to sit swinging, on a pile of cushions, whilst he received and chatted with his courtiers and guests.

The salute was fired and we hurried to our seats as the Maharaja's offerings of milk to the temple, "which is necessary for the worship of the gods," were carried past, under a kind of canopy by three attendants. The elephants, in festival array, marched slowly by, and the riderless horses. Then came troops and a standard captured from Tippu in his disastrous retreat out of Travancore; the Bodyguard; His Highness reclining in a beautiful palanquin of green and silver, followed by Brahmin officials in what is known as "temple dress." Stripped to the waist, with only the sacred cord over the shoulder, they wear a long white muslin skirt that folds round to the hips and is called a *dhoty*. It would be dishonour to the god to appear before him fully clothed, a rule that formerly applied to the men and even women servants of the palace, who had to drop their upper garment in the presence of royalty. This custom has now been discontinued.

The Maharaja is just twenty-three years old, slim of figure and good looking, with a refinement of features and physique that do not betoken strength. He too was in temple dress with simple white muslin draperies, but about his neck and naked breast glittered superb historic emeralds and diamonds.

His Highness ascended the throne three years ago, inheriting it through his mother, the Junior Maharani. She is the younger of two members of the Kolathunad family, a branch of the original Chera Kings. They were adopted by the late Maharaja for the reason that he had no sister to continue the line of succession. Their grand aunt took the mothers of these two ladies to Rameswaram, and at the Temple she solemnly vowed to adopt a daughter of each one of them, if and when they should be born.

The matriarchal system of inheritance prevails in the royal families of Cochin and Travancore and also among the Hindu caste of Nayars, who are only to be found on the Malabar coast, and are the soldiers of the race. A man's heir is never his own legitimate son, but the eldest male child of his sister. As an Indian proverb puts it: "Every man knows his own mother," and the arrangement was eminently suitable to ensure purity of descent amongst a people who practised polyandry, a custom that is now dying out.

The two Maharanis are cousins then, and the elder had no son, but she ruled as Regent during the seven years' minority of His Highness. To this day all domestic ceremonies of any importance take place at her official residence within the Fort, which she occupies as Senior Maharani.

The present ruler is a bachelor, and at no time would his marriage be of vital importance to Travancore. His sister's was celebrated with great magnificence a year ago, when the State guest houses were filled to overflowing and nothing of Eastern ceremonial was omitted; not even the *Nautch*, which was prohibited during the rule of the Senior Maharani, in connection with Temple rites. The radiant little lady and her consort are the ideal Prince and Princess of an eastern fairy tale. Her son, if the gods are kind, will be the heir apparent.

The late Maharaja enjoyed a long lease of life, and a reign of fifty-four years owing—it is said—to his extreme orthodoxy and that he continually lavished benefits on the Brahmins; who, possibly, hold the keys of life and death within their all-powerful grasp. Being orthodox, he was not progressive, and had never left the country, which made its appeal to the highest-caste Hindus and priests; whereas his successor has already crossed the seas and has travelled in Europe in the company of his mother. The gossips murmur that some temple treasures were sold to defray expenses, and this has given terrible offence in certain quarters.

During his minority His Highness spent a year in Bangalore studying administration, and a former Dewan was trained in the model State, so that as early in the century as 1904 the Prime Minister was able to announce that "Travancore is thus an object lesson of what a Hindu State, brought under the influence of enlightened and progressive ideas from the West, can achieve, without losing the distinctive character imprinted upon it." About that period, Lord Curzon, then Viceroy of India, had said: "The native chief has become by our policy an integral factor in the Imperial organization of India. He is concerned, not less than the Viceroy or the Lieutenant Governor, in the administration of the country. I claim him as my colleague and partner."

The *Dewan* of 1934 gave a large garden party to celebrate the Maharaja's birthday and his grounds were beautifully illuminated by electric lights; the principal piece being the Travancore coat of arms; a shield with three conch shells and supporters, two elephants. He is a Muhammedan and a widower, whose daughter-in-law lives with him. The lady is *purdah* but the Maharani refused to come to a house where the hostess would not be in evidence, so the curtain had to be lifted temporarily and be dropped again when the reception was over. The royal party had refreshments in a private room, but the rest of the guests, European men and women, Indian men and also Indian women, all had an English tea and ices in an immense apartment like a ballroom. It was my first and only experience of such a mingling of race and sex, illustrative of the superior social position and the greater freedom enjoyed by Nayar ladies and Syrian Christians. As pointed out to them at a meeting of the All India Women's Conference by Mrs. (Dr.) Reddi, they do not "suffer from the evil effects of child-marriage, early widowhood, or from unequal and unjust marriage laws and inheritance rights." To this higher civilization the Nambudri Brahmins, a distinct group of the priestly caste of Malabar, are still an exception. Their women are *purdah*, jealously guarded: the girls are married very young and in any case before puberty, on pain of excommunication and degradation from caste. Even amongst them, however, time is bringing about slowly a necessary reformation of their customs. At the *Dewan's* reception, I was interested to learn that the Nayar ladies usually wear white *saris* interwoven with wide gold lines, and also the Syrian Christians, who throw one end over the shoulder and it hangs down in fan shape, known as a "Cochin tail." They may change their *saris* as often as four times a day, and they sleep in the one they happen to be wearing at bedtime. Brahmin ladies preferably wear colours. Of any of them it might be said in the words of Sakuntala: [1]

> "A sweet Sirisha blossom should be twined
> Behind her ear, its perfumed crest depending
> Towards her cheek: and resting on her bosom
> A lotus fibre necklace, soft and bright
> As an autumnal moonbeam, should be traced."

The higher-caste Hindu and Christian women have excellent educational advantages at the imposing Women's College, planned by a former Dewan, whose sister was subsequently Head Mistress. The architecture is modern and severe; a crescent-shaped building divided in the centre by a pylon of Egyptian design. Within this entrance, hanging on the staircase, is an unflattering portrait of Her Highness the Senior Maharani, during whose Regency it was built. There is a large High School for girls and a Vernacular School within the Fort precincts, where only Brahmins and Nayars may live. The languages spoken are Malayalam and Tamil.

For boys and men there are Colleges of Science and of Arts, and a School of Arts where instruction is given in pottery and lacquer, carving in wood and ivory, and

[1] Translation by Monier Williams.

ARAT PROCESSION

the *Kufgari* work of steel inlaid with silver, only made in this part of India.

There is a Museum and a Public Library in which I spent many mornings, for it houses thirty thousand English books; literature of the past and present; modern novels; the best current newspapers and monthly journals.

Many of the public buildings are more like large gabled houses, and this makes Trivandrum a picturesque place, but it is "one that cannot be seen by any human eye" as a recent traveller very aptly remarked. This is true! I wished for a 'plane that never came to this out-of-the-way corner of the globe during my visit. Only by air could the town be seen to proper advantage, for the ground is undulating: many buildings, bungalows and houses are each on a hillock to their own benefit, but obstructing any views for the passer-by. Nothing could be better suited to the Nayar love of privacy. "The Englishman's home is his castle" would be far more applicable to a Nayar noble, living within his walled compound, with a small entrance cut into great gates under an archway. I was so fortunate as to be invited to one to see the family jewels. The front reception-rooms were furnished in the European style called "the bungalow." The women's quarters, beyond these, were practically empty, except for hammocks slung up in a corner, as they prefer amongst themselves to sit on mats on the floor. Many rooms are built round an oblong open to the sky over a cemented flooring about four, or more, inches deep with an outlet for the water, when it rains. The pillared supports to the roof of these apartments had quaintly carved capitals. There was also a strong room securely fastened with heavy iron clamps attached to the floor and wall. Life in these houses is very simple, and guests are always lodged in a separate building.

His Highness the Maharaja has just completed his new Kauviar Palace, a handsome three-storeyed mansion on a height, and with gardens surrounding it that, in this hot, damp air and with such fertile soil, will presently be very lovely. He had only been in residence a few days when I was commanded for an interview with him and H.H. the Junior Maharani, and I walked over a great length of marble-paved corridors to the drawing-rooms that have been furnished out of the West.

Her Highness questioned me about the Arat, which had taken place on the previous day. It is one of the most important festivals of the Hindu year in Travancore, and I had been permitted with friends to view it from a verandah of a disused palace on the line of route near the sea. Unfortunately the procession was delayed until very late in the afternoon, when the daylight was fading and we had all to go outside to the gates that we might be as near it as possible.

"Oh dear!" said the Maharani, with deepest disappointment in her voice, "then you could not see His Highness!" I hastened to assure her that, thanks to my unusual height, I had been able to look over the heads of the troops lining the road to the central figure of the Maharaja as he passed by. Treasure of her soul!

In token of his extreme humility and reverence the Maharaja, in temple dress, walks three miles from the Temple in the Fort to a *mantapam* on the shore, where he awaits the arrival of the gods, the Lord Sri Padmanabha, Narasimha and Sri Krishna, who are carried in state, and bathe in the sea with His Highness just after sundown.

The whole route was gaily decorated and the road strewn with fine white sand. During his long progress the Maharaja carried his unsheathed sword upright and also a shield. He was preceded by a sacred elephant with the flag and protected by his Nayar nobles in their ancient war kit, and by his bodyguard and palace staff armed with spears and shields as in days of old. His young brother, the Prince, followed closely in his footsteps. Then came attendants with a box containing a complete set of clothing for His Highness for his return in his brougham to the palace after the ceremonial bath: and another box with betel nut and flowers. The

Brahmin high officers of State were present in temple dress, and the Chief Secretary was a sick man for the remainder of my visit owing to the chill sea breeze.

There were musicians amongst the followers and a group of women, who serve the Temple, in white *saris*, carrying their little oil lamps like the wise and foolish virgins. The gods and their attendant priests were in the care of the sacred elephants, gorgeously caparisoned and wearing gold bosses: fourteen of them made a splendid show.

I had always thought that, apart from festival occasions, which indeed are frequent, these huge creatures must be horribly bored with their sacrosanct existence. It was a surprise to find that they are hired out for work sometimes, and as their hours are carefully regulated and must be adhered to, this must surely be a relief from the monotony of a temple cell.

Whilst we had been waiting for the procession, a member of the royal family, well known for his orthodox views and extreme piety, drove up to the gates of the palace in his brougham and, recognizing a friend in one of our party, alighted to have a chat. He was asked if we might be presented and his answer did not at all surprise me: "Yes, provided we did not shake hands," and at the same time he grasped his *dhoty* firmly with one hand, and his rosary with the other, to make any attempt to do so quite impossible. To touch any of us would have meant pollution and he must immediately have taken a bath before joining the procession, where we saw him, subsequently, fingering his beads and murmuring *mantras*. He is a very pious Hindu.

The late Maharaja of Travancore received his European guests before seven o'clock in the morning, and then bathed; the present Raja of Cochin, a very old man, holds his reception before he has his bath at 9 a.m.

It is the custom of our people.

Also I had heard the story of an incident that happened many years ago, when a distinguished British officer held out his hand to a high-caste Hindu, who drew back saying: "I cannot touch you to-day. I am holy just now. We are a very religious people, you know."

Travancore has been pre-eminently the "Land of Piety" since its consolidation under Martanda Varma the Great, who conquered the eight independent principalities of which the State originally consisted and made of them one Kingdom in 1750. In that year he dedicated it in perpetual endowment to the god of the Trivandrum Temple, Sri Padmanabha, as his feudal lord, and ruled it as servant of the family deity, who is an aspect of lotus-bearing Vishnu, with a conch shell in one of his four hands.

The Maharajas receive their plumed and jewelled turban with its aigrette of diamonds and emeralds, that is their crown, from the representatives of the god, the Brahmin priests of the Temple: also the sword of State and belt, "as the clearest possible acknowledgment of entire subservience." Themselves of the *Kshatriya* caste, the Rulers of Travancore must also perform a Temple ceremony that alone can place them on the same footing as the priestly caste and enable them to eat in company with Brahmins.

At the Arat procession my attention was especially attracted to the curious headdress worn by His Highness, that had two velvet tabs. These are symbolic that he is under the feet of the god, "the adorable feet of Venad," whose slave he is. The processional image of the Lord Sri Padmanabha is of gold, but the temple god —it is said—is very ancient and made of molasses cemented with a sort of glue, and was remade by order of Martanda Varma the Great.

It can be understood how keen was the anxiety and fear of devotees, shortly before my arrival at Trivandrum, when a fire broke out in the Temple which of all dangers that might befall a god made of molasses was, perhaps, the worst. The British, rigorously excluded as a rule from the sacred precincts, were allowed to go to the rescue, and the Lord Sri Padmanabha can only have been saved by a miracle, for the garland of a minor deity near by was badly scorched, and the outer corridor burnt.

A few evenings after the Arat, Her Highness the Junior Maharani very kindly invited me to the verandah of her palace that I might see another procession, which commemorates a hunting expedition of the Lord Sri Padmanabha, escorted by the Maharaja.

A tremendous crowd had assembled and I was glad when the police turned us out of the car on account of traffic regulations, and we were obliged to walk to the palace gates. This gave me the opportunity of taking a look at the shrine that had been erected just beyond them. It stood about five feet high by four wide and was composed of boughs and leaves. At the foot, slightly raised from the ground, were some coconuts.

It was a rather dark night and all taking part in the procession crept along barefooted with the utmost quietude and secrecy from the Temple to this shrine, as if stealthily tracking a wild beast.

The three gods arrived and were lined up in position facing the shrine. Then His Highness passed the gates armed with his bow. He walked up close to the coconuts and shot his arrow into them three times.

The silence was broken and the hunting party marched away, but as the gods had been present at a kill and were polluted by blood, they were unable to return to the Temple. They remained outside throughout the night and were replaced in their respective shrines at daybreak.

CHAPTER XVIII

THE ART OF PANTOMIME AND DANCE

"A great master of dancing is Siva! The cosmos is his theatre, there are many different steps in his repertory, he himself is actor and audience."

"When the Actor beateth the drum
Everybody cometh to see the show:
When the Actor collecteth the stage properties
He abideth alone in his happiness."

On one of my sightseeing days in Trivandrum itself, I wandered into the precincts of the Fort and discovered much more of interest than I had anticipated, for I was well aware that I should not be admitted into the Temple, which is the principal and most picturesque building within the enclosure. Recently, a distinguished guest of the State, when asked what she particularly wished to see, had included temples in her list, but that suggestion was definitely blue-pencilled by the Maharani. So I had to content myself by strolling round about the pagoda of the Lord Sri Padmanabha, when I came unexpectedly upon a sentry; and, farther on, discovered the Maharaja's palace staff in their quaint garb, which begins at the waist and consists mainly of shields and spears entirely in keeping with these grim walls, barred courts and dark mysteries. His Highness, it seemed, had just arrived for morning *puja*.

Then a kind friend offered to take me into the Vernacular Record Office and within high gates we found a Nayar dwelling (in appearance) with gabled roof, and passed through several offices into the open air, and finally arrived at a large barred shed. In it are housed the temple accounts of past years; title deeds of property; important transactions of State written in Malayalam, or Tamil, with a pointed steel instrument on dried palm

DEVADASIS

THE KUMMIE DANCE AT THE TRICHUR SCHOOL

leaves. The strips varied in length according to the required size, from about two and a half to four feet, tied together in large bundles that were piled up to the roof. I contemplated them in silent stupefaction, struck by the idea that the difficulty of tracing any details after long years was only equalled by the facility with which such records might be tampered with. In fact, the present Keeper, recently appointed, almost put my feelings into so many words.

From the Record Office we went on to the Vernacular School for Girls. They acted for us: the same drama again that is such a favourite, Krishna and the Milkmaids. The child, who played the mischievous boy god, coloured her face blue for her rôle, but there was no dressing-up apart from that. Mounted on a stool, Krishna scolded the *gopis* for pursuing him and they were all very tearful, dancing round him with sad faces.

After that was over, a group of girls, clothed much alike in *sari* skirts and yellow jackets, gave a performance of a difficult and strenuous dance with many complicated steps and very tiring. There was a great deal of hand- and foot-work, but they never flagged and seemed to be enjoying themselves immensely. It was a folk dance they gave us of the Nayar women, which commemorates the death of the Hindu Cupid, Kama Deva, on a certain date about the beginning of January. The five arrows from the god's sugar-cane bow, then temporarily at rest, are made from the lotus, asoka, mango, jasmine and blue lily, for his friend and ally is the spring. The girls, big and little, make a gay festival of it, turn night into day singing special songs and dancing round a lighted lamp till dawn.

It has been said of Malabar that it is the Museum of India, and this especially applies to arts of mind and body, rather than to handicrafts. Old customs have lingered. It is the home of tradition and drama, folk dance and pantomime; of the action-song invented by Kunjan Nambyar, a "poet of genius." Forgotten, lost, destroyed, relegated to the dust-heap of the Ages in other parts of

India, in Travancore, Cochin and the West Coast, these arts have been preserved and perfected with all the Indian love of detail to excess. Now a great revival is taking place, a searching of museum shelves for the best that has ever been, by initiative of the blind poet, Valathol, and of the great Pavlova's dancing partner in her Hindu ballet; by Uday Shankar, a Brahmin of Udaipur.

An artist to his finger-tips, Shankar went to London to study as a painter, under the direction of Rothenstein, who recognized his gifts and advised him to follow the lines of Indian art, of which the great master is an admirer. In the meantime, the enthusiastic pupil had fallen at the feet of Pavlova and had been sent by her to the British Museum to copy the décor and costume of the Krishna Raj for her ballet. His studies were a revelation to him of the wonders of his own country, but he quickly realized that modifications must be made in its expression to render Eastern dancing acceptable to Western minds. Also, that in the course of centuries decadence has crept into the symbology, which is the *raison d'être* of an Indian dance, born of the Hindu cult, the worship of the gods.

"Saraswati plays on the *vina*, Indra on the flute, Brahma holds the time-marking cymbals, Lakshmi begins a song, Vishnu plays on a drum . . . and all the beings in the three worlds assemble there to witness the celestial dance and to hear the music of the divine choir at the hour of twilight." It is Siva as Nataraja, who is the magical dancer in the Dance of Life and the *joie de vivre* is apparent in every pose. Eternally he dances with grace, harmony and rhythm. In his hands he holds a drum, symbol of the Universe and a ball of flame for purity. "He dances with Water, Fire, Wind and Ether. Thus our Lord dances ever in the Court."

Brahmin and artist, Uday Shankar deplores the fact that Mysore State suppressed the temple dances of the *devadasis* in 1909, an example followed by H.H. the Senior Maharani of Travancore when Regent, and by Cochin. Now in Baroda, Savantwadi and elsewhere, strenuous efforts are being made to prohibit the age-old custom of dedicating girls of eight and nine years old to the State Temples for the service of the gods. "If an entire abolition of the system," he says, "means giving a final blow to the beautiful art of the Hindu *nautch*, it must give us pause."

> "The dancing foot, the sound of the tinkling bells,
> The songs that are sung and the varying steps."

> "When, oh my beloved, wilt thou return? delight of my heart and treasure of my soul?
> I am scented with the oils of Lahore and tinged with the blossoms of henna; haste then, my beloved, to thine handmaid, gladden her heart by thy presence."
>
> *A Song of the Nautch.*

Parents often dedicate a girl to the Temple to ensure her recovery from sickness; or else, that a son may be born to them if they have no male offspring. Again, if they are poor, they will gladly sell their child for a sum that depends on her age and beauty; or, a *devadasi* will take her on the adoption system. If she tries to escape, she is branded under the arm and whipped. The children are highly trained in the arts of singing, dancing and obscenity and as gifts to the god they are, in practice and by right, gifts to the Sivaite and Vishnavaite priests who serve the Temples. Vested interests in prostitution jealously guard temple rights. "As long as the *nautch* is fashionable amongst us and freely indulged in," says Dr. Bandarkar, "it is impossible that the morality of men should greatly improve, or that our respect for women in any way increase."

The *devadasis* have charge of the outer door of the Temple and open it daily. They burn camphor, or carry the sacred light and do *puja* before the god; mount the cars at festivals; fan the idol with Thibetan ox-tails; sing and dance before it at processions: "creatures of naught but fantasy and pleasure."

Uday Shankar's fears that these twin arts may lapse and die out seems to me quite groundless, whilst there are twelve thousand *devadasis* trained for the *nautch* in

British South India alone, where nothing will be done to put a stop to their profession. No action would ever be taken that "could be interpreted as a breach of that religious neutrality, which is one of the cardinal principles of British rule in India." The Government has "a tender regard for the alleged religious susceptibilities of the Hindu": moreover, when parents not only actively encourage their daughters to practise prostitution, but force them into it as young children, there certainly is no remedy.

It is the custom of our people: that suffices.

In his lecture, which I have just quoted in respect to the *nautch*, Shankar ignored the Tiruvathirakali of Travancore, and the *Kolattam* and *Kummie* folk dances of Tamil villages, now being taught in the vernacular and mission schools of South India. They also have their origin in the religion of the people and in sun worship, and are transformed into play songs for little Christians. The *Kummie* is in reality an ecstatic hymn to Vishnu who, as Narayana, resides in the great celestial orb.

"Hail! Hail to thee supreme ruler of the world.
Lord! All hail to thee, who hath destroyed Paka, Hail!
Hail to thee, who surpass in beauty the God of Love.
Hail! Hail to thee, chiefest among Gods.
We worship thee."

"O celestial daughters, beautifully shaped, we must compose dances of still greater beauty.
Come! Let us rejoice most excellently the heart of Paka's enemy.
Oh Indulekha! dearest, dance with the divine grace that is famous in Indra's palace.
Oh Rambha! thou, fairest among women, sing us a song
In low sweet tones, oh beloved!"[1]

Though H.H. the Senior Maharani of Travancore wiped out the *nautch* with a stroke of her pen, the temples do not lack dancers, but they are men versed in the art of pantomime and good story-tellers, the Thullals. Welcomed at all the great festivals they entertain a delighted audience with tales from the Puranas. Like

[1] A. Meerwarth, *Journal Asiatique*, 1926.

our music-hall artists, they are allowed considerable licence to interlard these with topical allusions, witticisms and sarcasms about well-known local people and current events. A Thullal may even indulge in invectives about those present and none can say him nay.

My interest in these Chakyars, as they are often called, was aroused by an actor who came to the hotel to be photographed, by request, together with his two musicians, who always are with him; one to lead the song, the other to accompany and beat time with his drum.

On the first occasion, the Thullal wore an outstanding ballet skirt of two-inch-wide white ribbons edged with rose pink: on the other, a skirt with light-coloured drapery like a scarf tied in a huge bow in front with the ends hanging. He had a wonderful head-dress.

We were told a story of a Brahmin who prayed to Siva for wealth, but as he never cast his eyes on the ground (with humility) he missed seeing the gold and silver coins that the god strewed plentifully on his path; so remained a poor and disappointed man all his days.

The tale was expressed by song and wonderful dumb show of the actor, whose gestures and especially the poses of hands and fingers are the result of highly developed study. "The Thullals follow a time-honoured form and technique of their art, from which they do not permit of any deviation."

This can be said, even more truly, of the Kathakalis, actors of the old-world drama of Malabar, who originated with a Raja of the early seventeenth century, a vague, shadowy person of whom nothing else seems to be known. They have their own freemasonry, and when two members meet they fall at each other's feet and exchange salutations, using language peculiar to themselves. The long, strenuous training they receive is so specialized and so exact in every particular, that members of one troupe can join another and immediately fall into place without rehearsal. Such perfection is only possible after fifteen years of hard work and I was fortunate in getting a brief insight into their methods, at the

School for Kathakalis at Trichur, under the direction of the poet Valathol.

It was after my visit to Lake Periyar that I went forty miles farther afield than was warranted on a return journey to Trivandrum, and stayed a few days at this ancient Brahmin town, one-time capital of Cochin State. Tippu had made it his headquarters when he swept through Malabar and its fortress temple sustained a Muslim siege. Its architecture is quite unlike that of any other pagoda I had seen and peculiar to Travancore. It is more like a three-storeyed mansion with overhanging gabled roofs and the large walled-in enclosure has a high *gopuram* for each point of the compass, but not one entrance by which I could be admitted. Here the most exclusive Brahmin sect, the Nambudris, have a sacred training college for priests. Novices dwell there for years alone and in silent meditation, fixing the mind on some object well defined in space to attain sanctity.

But, after all, it was not the temple that had attracted me to Trichur, nor students of passivity and inanition, but the Kathakalis, the exponents of rhythmic energy, whose school I found five miles outside the town.

An unexpected visitor, I arrived in the morning about half-past ten, to find that the pupils had been at work since 4.30 a.m. They begin their day with physical drill to keep their limbs supple and attain the perfect control and balance of the body that is a necessity of their art and constitutes its charm. They sit round a fire, the light playing on their features, to learn facial expression and the language of the lips and eyes. Fear is expressed by constant moving of the eyeballs, a jerking of head and neck, the hands folded on the breast: wonder by quivering eyebrows and nodding: wrath by wide-open eyes, fiery, piercing eyeballs, throbbing cheeks, occasional biting of the lips.

There is an alphabet of dumb show with palms and fingers that takes years to acquire: hand poses that are sixty-four in number and of these four are in constant use, each one with sixteen ideas of its own. Gestures

THE OTTAM THULLAL

are of three kinds: entirely natural and produced unconsciously; imitative; or symbolic of ritual, worship, benediction and offering to the gods. "As this art is justified by nature, so also is nature embellished by this art." It is the study of a lifetime and a boy is enrolled for training at the age of from twelve to fourteen, by payment of a sum in cash, or by a gift of clothes to the instructor.

I found a little group of lads assembled in the schoolroom, which was merely a large shed open at both sides, roofed-in and with a stone flooring. The furniture consisted of a table and a bench, which was being utilized to represent a child's cot at the moment of my arrival; for I had chanced upon the Krishna legend again, and this time, the beginning of the story. As a young child, his life was threatened by the Herod of Hinduism, to whom it had been predicted that his own existence was endangered by the birth of a miraculous child to a certain woman, seven of whose children had already been put to death by the tyrant.

When I made my appearance, an advanced pupil was receiving very specialized instruction in the rôle of the demoness sent to poison Krishna with bread and molasses. It was most interesting to watch the play of the eyes, of every feature, of every gesture, all expressive of coaxing and calming a rather frightened child and the effort to soothe and win its confidence.

Two musicians lent their aid to the performance: gestures were emphasized by the drummer and elaborated by the pupil to the fullest extent of his powers but not always with success. Now and again the accomplished instructor would get up from his stool and show how this movement should be made, these fingers given their full meaning; for the dramaturgy of Bharata Natya Sastra is standardized and no alteration is allowed.

The lesson finished, I went into another building to examine the wonderful armlets, anklets, necklets and chest ornaments renovated, or newly made, for a forthcoming tour of a troupe in Burma. Gold leaf was being applied to furbish up some; fresh, coloured glass inserted where precious gems were lacking; new tinkling bells added to the wide bands that encircle the legs of the actor-dancer in his manifestation of the primal energy that never tires.

Head-dresses were most elaborate, made on a frame of light wood and decorated with glass and spangles and little glistening bits of mirror. A god could be identified by a wide gold halo, like a plate: a monkey if the dancer wears a white beard and a demon by a large, swarthy hirsute appendage covering all the chin and half the cheeks.

Of equal importance is the make-up, and I also visited the cosmetic specialists and saw them at work preparing the rice flour, which is made into paste and thickly plastered over the whole face, where it dries and hardens. There is no idea of imitating, or improving upon nature, but the colour applied, whether pale green, red, yellow, black or white, is significant of a certain person, or of a type. Brahmins, saints and sages have yellow and red; Krishna, or some other Great One is green, and the god wears a black jacket; the dancer with a red beard and coat, a red face picked out with black round eyes, lips and chin is Bali, the monkey demon-king. The eyes of all are reddened with the seed of Solanum.

Costumes are elaborate and it is curious that the dress and make-up of women resembles that of the Moplahs of Malabar, who are Muslims, but the Kathakalis are always youths or men; women are rigorously excluded.

Time was when every wealthy high-caste family had their own troupe of players: thirty men, of whom twelve were actors, four were singers, four were drummers, and the rest, attendants and servants. Nowadays, only H.H. the Maharaja has his private company of Kathakalis.

One evening I was so fortunate as to be bidden to the Palace of the late Maharaja, where a hall had been built on to and enclosing a long stone balcony, that was the only auditorium. The Dramas are played always after sunset and the invitation was for half-past six o'clock.

We sat in one long row facing the actors, who were on the ground-level. There was no stage, or scenery, and the accessories were of the simplest, for everything depends on characterization. Two large standard coconut-oil lamps illuminated the players, and were fed and trimmed from time to time by attendants when the yellow flames burned low.

The Drama was from the Mahabharata and entitled "The Killing of King Duryodhana," which conveyed nothing to me until I had read a typed summary of the seven scenes and discovered it was an incident in the lives of the Pandava Brothers and Draupadi.

The eldest Pandava, King Dharmaputhra, intended performing an animal sacrifice, a *Yaga* on a grand scale, and invited his cousins, the Kauravas, to his Court to witness it. His architect, Maya, had constructed an artificial fountain in front of the palace, which was of a magical character. It was in two parts, one full of water and one dry, but no one could tell the one from the other. Unfortunately the Kaurava King walked into the water, spoiling his best clothes, and all his suite fell in after him. Draupadi thought this a great joke and burst out laughing loudly, so that Duryodhana, her guest, was insulted and furious at her conduct. He vowed to be revenged.

A large white cloth held up on supports by two boys did duty as a curtain and from behind it came the beating of *tom-toms* and the music of cymbals and the conch. When removed, the play began with a gambling scene between the two Kings. A Kaurava courtier loaded Duryodhana's dice, so that he soon won everything from Dharmaputra, his kingdom, and at the last Draupadi, his beautiful wife. Now the Kaurava King could wreak his vengeance on the woman who had insulted him. He sent for her and one of his wicked courtiers dragged her in by the hair and strove to untie the knot that fastened her *sari* that he might outrage her before them all. Draupadi, who was very devout, prayed for help from Sri Krishna, so that her garments grew more voluminous and longer and the knot defied all efforts to loosen it. Then she vowed that never would she unfasten it again, until her husband, Bhima, the second Pandava Brother, should kill the wicked courtier and untie the knot for her with his blood-stained hands.

The Pandavas had always enjoyed the favour of this powerful god and now implored him to undertake a mission on their behalf to the capital of the Kauravas. In Scene VI we witnessed Sri Krishna's arrival at court and how he made himself known, so that devotees fell at his feet and worshipped him.

As a result the cousins went to war with each other, and I think it was at this juncture that the Pandavas recovered their arms from the sacred tree, where they were hidden, which is commemorated at the Mysore Dasara. But this did not come into the play.

In the last scene the eldest brother had regained his kingdom and was crowned in the presence of the family god.

Usually a Kathakali drama takes from eight to nine hours in its performance, necessitating a relay of actors. On this occasion the play had obviously been condensed, and about the end of the fifth scene the Maharaja sent for the Brahmin priest, who was stage manager and gave some instructions. I gathered from H.H. the Junior Maharani, who was seated on my right and who had been most kind in explaining the incidents to me that might puzzle a foreigner, that the play had been further cut down. Moreover, I thought that the excessive beating of the *tom-toms*, the blowing of the conch had also been lessened out of consideration for the susceptibility of Western ears. Yet the symbology had been perfect, since every day the Dance of Life becomes more noisy, the vibrations of the spheres more strident for all the world. It is the will of the magical dancer. "Thus our Lord dances ever in the Court."

PHYSICAL DRILL BY STUDENTS AT TRICHUR

CHAPTER XIX

LAND'S END

"A bird flew over the pine-clad hill
  Of the old, old legends singing,
And carried me out of life's beaten way
  Into dreamland's dim beginning."

"Then trembled the three worlds and all the Earth
With ocean, islands, mountains, deserts quailed
And then upon the string that arrow dread
That, winged with flames, burns awful, like the fire
Of the great day of doom . . .
And all the waters of the ocean boiled."

THOUGH never in doubt, when I passed into Travancore, that I had entered a Wonderland of fable and fancy, yet as the normal European life began to flow around and draw me into the official social circle of its capital, I became less conscious of it (with stray glimpses of Oriental imagery), until I started on my way to Cape Comorin. Then it gripped me again and at Land's End held me fast.

The whole of the beautiful, interesting drive of fifty-four miles is punctuated with innumerable legends, that account in some strange way for accidents of landscape; or are born out of geographical conditions, subsidence and upheaval in a far-away, vague past; or due to animistic worship and dread of Nature inherent in all primitive peoples, until the lonely traveller becomes mentally steeped in the realization that all this West Coast country, from Goa to Cape Comorin, has been the ocean bed, rescued by some miracle from the depths of the sea about 2,300 years B.C. How, then, could it be like the rest of the world, or its inhabitants (who were literally pulled into it by the hair of their heads), quite like the rest of mankind?

Geologists may talk as they please in explanation of the disappearance and re-appearance of Kerala, or Malabar, fifteen hundred miles long by one hundred and fifty wide and account for it as volcanic action. The people have another tale to tell of the great Aryan warrior, Parasurama, sixth incarnation of Vishnu, "Rama of the Axe."

It is recorded in the Brahmanda Purana that the sons of Sagara dug a hole and descended into hell in quest of a horse stolen by Indra and deposited there. They were burned by the fire of Kapila's wrath; all the country round sank into the ocean and with it, to the infinite distress of devotees, the great temple of Gokarnum (Goa).

Now it happened that Parasurama had been waging war against the *Kshatriyas* and had well-nigh destroyed them, whereupon he was filled with remorse and gave away his kingdom to Brahma. Left, then, without a country to rule over, he regretted his hasty action and appealed to the sea god for another. His request was granted and he begged permission to reclaim all that land up to the point to which he could hurl his battle-axe, thrown into the sea from where he stood at Goa. His weapon fell on Land's End, a rocky, barren promontory at the junction of the Arabian Sea and the Gulf of Mannar; therefore sacred to the Hindu mind. By order of the god, the waters receded, land was thrown up; all the West Coast of Malabar, Cochin and Travancore to make a kingdom for Parasurama, but uninhabited by man.

A ruler without subjects, the doughty Aryan imported them from one place and another: from the Krishna River he brought Brahmins, their wives and families, and settled them at Trichur, a town of great antiquity. From Tanjore others arrived to people twenty-four villages, but they were discontented and fled back again, declaring the country to be unhealthy, full of swamps and snakes.

He adopted the more drastic measures I have already mentioned, and as may be seen to this day by the sacred, unshaven lock of the Nambudri Brahmins, pulled forward on their heads unlike all others of the elect. He settled them as petty sovereigns with a new language,

Malayalam, and innovations of custom and habit that would keep them rooted to earth as the traditional landowners. They are held in great reverence as an exclusive sect of Brahmins peculiar to Malabar, a socio-spiritual aristocracy.

Malabar became a "Land of good works for the expiation of sin" with twelve kingships, aptly described by the Malayalam proverb, "Though two steps might be made in one territory, a third must pass the boundary line."

Nature's drama was followed by the romance of the Virgin Goddess at Cape Comorin and of the Royal House of Travancore by the disappearance of the last of the Perumals, that mysterious Raja who vanished from his stone sleeping-cot at a period of history as vague and fascinating as himself; of the vicissitudes of the great Martanda Varma, who consolidated the State in 1335 and is remembered as the saviour of Travancore; of Raja Varma, the first Travancore painter of note; of Kulasekhara Perumal Rama Varma, G.C.S.I., created Maharaja by the British in recognition of his excellent administration in 1866; of the present ruler, now in enjoyment of the interlude of youth.

All the countryside in that long drive to the Cape from Trivandrum is eloquent of the unusual and the landscape is one of infinite variety. At the start, with the thermometer at 85° F., it is true that the dense foliage of the coconut palms was somewhat oppressive and the recurring paddy fields kept the atmosphere humid as well. Herein are the sources of beauty and fertility, together with three lovely shaded tanks; one called "Gold," since its value to the people is above all baser metal, and where a goddess was transfixed on the roadside bank by a magician; and yet another within the first eighteen miles of Trivandrum, "The Tank without Frogs."

To account for this phenomenon the people have an allegory of some historical episode and they say that there were many frogs at one time, who had a king of their own species. But they grew tired of him and chose an alligator as raja, who gave them pick-a-back rides, which they loved, so he was crowned by unanimous consent. He was so kind and condescending that he let them hop into his huge cavern of a mouth and explore it, but after a while they discovered that they were rapidly diminishing in numbers. It was too late, and not one was left to croak the tragic story.

A few miles farther on, where the soil, and consequently also the scene changes, there would be no smiling paddy fields had not man come to the rescue of Nature, as long ago as 900 A.D., and constructed a dam that turned a desert into cultivable land. In more arid soil tapioca grows, food of the poorest; and instead of graceful, spreading coconut palms, another variety, tall and scrubby trees that shame their kindred by their unhandsome looks. But they are equally useful: to make palmyra fans, basketwork, for thatching, mat-making and also for sustaining food and drink, white sugar and sweetmeats from the jaggery that the palmyra palms produce in great quantities.

It was after this stage of the drive that I told the chauffeur to leave the main road and take me to Eraniel, that I might see the ancient residence of the Travancore kings before they took up their residence within the precincts of Padmanabhapuram Fort, capital of Martanda Varma, thirty-three miles south of Trivandrum. I had a fancy to see the pillared stone cot from which Cheraman Perumal so mysteriously vanished that some say he was translated to heaven; some, that he turned Muhammedan and went to Mecca; and some, that he wandered off into the jungle and became a Buddhist monk.

The tale, which dates back to 333 A.D., naturally varies with the personal belief of the narrator and the district in which it is told. In Malabar, where Arabs intermarried with women of the coast, there remains a breed of Moplahs, fanatical Muslims, who relate a vision of the partition of the moon, which prompted Cheraman Perumal to seek Mahomet. He embarked secretly on a ship and escaped to Arabia, where he married the king's sister and was canonized by the Prophet as "Crown of the Faith." Within the past year a Muslim pilgrim returned to Travancore and spread about a story that he had seen the tomb and mosque of the lost prince—whose memory still lives in the hearts of his people.

The Portuguese had known of the mystery of Eraniel, for their poet Camoens gave his version of it in the Lusiad:

> "Having no heir, left the royal house.
> Before he parted he did cantonize
> His realm. Those servants he loved best, he brings
> From want to wealth, from subjects to be kings."

Presently the car stopped at a wide greensward with a few stone steps that obviously led to the ancient palace, indicated by its enclosing walls and high barred gates. I peered between the iron railings and could just catch a glimpse of an extensive, gabled dwelling, but neither persuasion, nor bribe, would turn the great key; so jealously and with such hostility the place was guarded. Half the village turned out to assist at the animated parley which ensued. I was told that it might be possible to obtain a permit to view from the local magistrate, but he was a Christian and had never been allowed within himself. That would be a hopeless quest.

When I spoke of my disappointment, subsequently, at Trivandrum, I was told that the real reason of my non-admittance was due to the fact that a temple adjoins the palace, but there is no doubt that the bedchamber itself is sacred and a lamp has been kept alight beside the cot throughout the centuries. Moreover, until the coronation of the present Maharaja, it had been the custom for each new ruler of the State to vow, as he received the State sword from the priests: "I will keep this sword until the uncle who has gone to Mecca returns again."

The farther south, the more ancient and undying the beliefs! When Parasurama's second set of colonists were pulled into Travancore by the hair, they found that the serpent gods were in possession of the partly reclaimed land and war broke out between them. With diplomatic tact, the Aryan warrior issued an edict of propitiation, whereby a corner of every compound should be set apart, and the undergrowth left untouched as an abode for the snakes, and at Nagercoil, the largest town on the road to Cape Comorin, the Hindu Temple has a shrine to Ananta, the serpent god. Every year a Nambudri Brahmin, celebrated for his power over cobras, comes there from North Travancore to perform *puja*.

Where there is serpent worship it is nearly always true that also there has been Buddhism, and this seems to have been the case at Suchindram if one may be allowed to judge by the construction of the "four-wheeled image car," which stood outside the temple in readiness for the December festival, superintended by Government officials, as it is of great importance to the State.

Though not an admirer of Hindu architecture, that is too baroque and overcrowded for my taste, Suchindram, at least one thousand years old, about ten miles from Land's End, was very arresting; possibly on account of its great antiquity. Here Siva dwells and the legend of his coming is closely linked up with the Temple at the Cape, home of the Virgin Goddess, Kumari, the Forsaken Bride.

For more than half the latter part of the drive, after coconut palms had been left behind, hills had altered the scene, especially the isolated Maha Indra, where Hanuman collected herbs for the wounded of Rama's supporters in search of Sita. In this region coffee was once cultivated, but has now been superseded by tea. Farther on, an irrigation canal came into sight, and all around the Fort of Martanda Varma's capital the ground was picturesque and rocky as far as Udaygiri. From there to Nagercoil, to feed its population of 40,000, there were wondrous paddy fields that yield two crops per year, with a background of mountain range that only finishes where the axe of the fable cleft the waters at India's seventh, sacred place of pilgrimage.

Poor goddess! A marriage had been arranged for

AN ITINERANT MUSICIAN, TRAVANCORE

A TYPICAL SCENE IN SOUTH TRAVANCORE

her with Siva. The wedding day found her expectant of his arrival after sundown. Only when darkness has fallen may the nuptials of the gods take place. The feast was ready and the bride; yet Siva came not.

Deeply concerned, Kumari ventured forth a weary way to meet her lagging bridegroom, and stood so long on a rock awaiting him that the impress of her foot is indelible in the stone.

Hour after hour passed: the long procession of the night went slowly by, and as the dawn broke, Kumari fled back to her sanctuary, knowing herself unwedded to the end of Time.

Siva had been delayed, but at last he reached Suchindram, only seven miles away. Too late! It was day and the cock crew. He was forced to take refuge in the Temple where he dwells for evermore.

The angry goddess flung all the wedding supper out on to the beach in a frenzy of wild despair. When my car stopped at the guest-house, it was at once surrounded by old women with baskets filled with fragments that they tried to sell to me. Heaps of rice fossilized into chalcedonic quartz; chilis that are now rolled garnet; balls of black pepper for seasoning that the geologists insist on calling iron ore. Grains of sand, but such a multiplicity of shapes and colours that the shores of Cape Comorin are said to be almost unique in India.

Strolling along on this wondrous beach at the mystic hour of sunset, a *pujari* offered his services as guide to the Temple enclosures.

Without, stand four stone monoliths, twenty feet in height, to attract the Evil Eye—perhaps lightning—away from the pagoda founded by Parasurama. They are emblematic of the four castes; the four rigid pillars of the Hindu social and religious edifice that have upheld the wheel of the Hindus' world for countless generations. A wheel that "turns through a full circle and always brings them back to the point from which they started."

FINIS

BIBLIOGRAPHY

Behind Mud Walls . . .	Charlotte and W. H. Wiser.
Castes and Tribes of Southern India	Edgar Thurston.
Chingleput District and its Antiquarian Remains	T. S. Venkatesan.
Crux of the Indian Problem, The .	R. P. Paranjpye, M.A., D.Sc.
Hindu Holidays and Ceremonials .	Rai Bahadur, B.A. Gupte R.S.A., F.Z.S., etc.
Hindu Religious Year, The . .	M. M. Underhill.
History of Indian and Eastern Architecture	James Fergusson.
History of Mysoor	Colonel Mark Wilks.
History of the Nayaks of Madura .	R. Sathyanatha Aiyar, M.A., L.T.
India: Its Life and Thought. .	J. P. Jones, D.D.
India through the Ages. . .	Jadeenath Sarkar, M.A., C.I.E.
Life in an Indian Village . .	T. Ramakrishna, B.A.
Mahabharata	J. M. Macfie, M.A.
My Experiences as a Legislator .	Mrs. (Dr.) S. M. Reddi.
Mysore, Gazetteer of . . .	Lewis Rice.
Myths and Legends of India . .	J. M. Macfie, M.A.
Omens and Superstitions . .	Edgar Thurston.
Phrenologist among the Todas, A .	Colonel W. E. Marshall.
Position of Women in Indian Life, The	H.H. Maharani of Baroda and S. M. Mitra.
Rites of the Twice-Born, The .	Mrs. Sinclair Stevenson.
Setu and Rameswaram, The . .	N. Vanamamalai Pillai.
Surya-Siddhânta . . .	Trans. Rev. E. Burgess.
Todas, The	W. H. R. Rivers.
Travancore.	E. G. Hatch.

Underworld of India, The . .	Lieut.-Gen. Sir George McMunn, K.C.B., K.C.S.I., D.S.O.
Village Gods of South India, The	Rt. Rev. H. Whitehead, D.D.
Web of Indian Life, The . .	Sister Nivedita (Margaret Noble).

GLOSSARY

Amnôr	The Toda Heaven.
Amrita	Drink of the gods.
Anna	Small nickel coin (a fraction over 1*d*.).
Ashram	Religious school and hostel.
Avatar	Incarnation in another form.
Ayurvedic	Science of life.
Baksheesh	A tip.
Banni	A sacred tree, prosopis spicegera.
Baniya	Caste of traders, moneylenders.
Bel tree	Wood apple, sacred to Siva.
Bengalu	A sort of bean.
Betel	Pepper plant.
Brahmahatya	Murder of a Brahmin.
Brahmanas	Writings 800–500 B.C.
Brahmin	Highest Hindu caste (sprung from the mouth of Brahma, the Creator).
Caste (*Portuguese*)	Colour [bar].
Chota	Small (lit.). Early breakfast (also chota hazri).
Choultry	Indian guest-house.
Chunam [*plaster*]	Calcined shells and limestone.
Crore	100 lakhs: 10 millions.
Deva	God.
Devadasi	Temple dancing girl and prostitute.
Dewan	Prime Minister.
Dhobi	Washerman (low caste).
Dhoty	Long muslin skirt worn by men.
Fakir	Holy man.
Garuda	Kite, favourite vehicle of Vishnu.
Ghat	Landing stair (lit.), Mountain road.
Ghi	Clarified butter.
Gold mohur	Tree with crimson flowers.
Gosha	Behind the curtain.
Guru	A holy man.

Harijan . . . Beloved of God (lit.). One of the depressed classes.

Jambuka . . . Rose-apple tree.
Jaya . . . Victory.
Jilebis . . . Sweets made chiefly of ghi.
Jutka . . . Indian pony-cart.

Kalasam . . . Gold coronal of a shrine.
Khaddar . . . Homespun.
Kharma . . . Fate to be worked out by each individual.
Kolam . . . Diagram drawn on the threshold in rice-powder.
Kolattam . . . Marching song, dance.
Koubba (*Arabic*) . Tomb of a saint.
Kshatriya . . . Second main caste of Hindus (sprung from the arms and body of Brahma). Military.
Kummie . . . Folk dance of the women.

Lakh . . . 100,000.
Lal Bagh . . . Red garden (lit.), used for parks and large gardens.
Linga, lingam . . Phallic symbol of Siva.

Mahabharata . . Epic poem 500 B.C.–A.D. 400.
Mahatma . . . A person possessed of supernatural powers, supposed to exist in India and Thibet. A Hindu holy man.
Mahout . . . Elephant driver.
Maidan . . . Large open space of waste ground.
Manu, Laws of . . 200 B.C.–A.D. 200.
Mantapam . . . Pillared hall.
Mantra, Mantram . A prayer, a text.
Mar (*Syriac*) . . Lord, saint.
Margosa (*or Neem tree*) Sacred tree, evergreen, white flowers.
Math . . . Charitable dispensary.
Monsoon . . . The rainy season.
Munsiff . . . Village magistrate.
Musnud . . . Throne of a raja.

Nandi . . . Bull, vehicle of Siva.
Nautch . . . Dance by Indian women.
Neem tree (*or Margosa*) Temple tree, evergreen, bearing white flowers
Nilgiris . . . Blue hills.

Odeanam . . . Belt.

Parcherry . . .	Quarter of village assigned to outcastes.
Pariah . . .	Outcaste.
Pavadar . . .	Dress of very young unmarried girl.
Peepal . . .	A sacred tree.
Perumal . . .	Divinity, goddess.
Pie, pice . . .	Small copper coins.
Pongal . . .	Sweetened cooked rice. Spring festival.
Puggaree . . .	Turban.
Puja . . .	Worship.
Pujari . . .	Priest in temple of female deity.
Pundit . . .	Learned man.
Puranas . . .	Myths A.D. 400–A.D. 800.
Purdah . . .	Curtain (lit.). Used to describe high caste Muhammedan and Hindu ladies always hidden away.
Purohits . . .	Priests.
Ragi	Red (lit.). Grain eaten by the poor.
Raja	Monarch, prince.
Ramayana . . .	Epic poem 500 B.C.
Rani	Queen, princess.
Rathas . . .	Temple cars.
Rishi . . .	A sage.
Rupee . . .	Silver coin (about 1*s.* 6*d.*).
Sadhu . . .	Hindu ascetic, holy man.
Salagrama . . .	Household fetish, symbol of Vishnu, often an ammonite, or curved stone.
Sunyasi, n . .	Hindu holy man.
Sari (*s.*), *saris* (*pl.*) .	Woman's dress.
Sati	Woman who immolates herself on her husband's funeral pyre.
Sesha . . .	Many-headed cobra on which Vishnu reclines during his four months' sleep.
Setu	Bridge, causeway.
Setubandha . .	Ocean bridge of Rama.
Shikari . . .	Big-game hunter.
Shradha . . .	Death ceremonies.
Soma . . .	Plant mentioned in the Rigveda.
Sri	St., saint.
Sudra . . .	Lowest (fourth) caste of Hindus (sprung from the feet of Brahma).
Sufi	Muslim sect.
Surya-Siddhânta . .	Established conclusion.
Swami . . .	A monk, a saint, a god.
Swastika . . .	Cross with bent arms (freemasonry).

Tahsildar . . .	Sub-divisional magistrate.
Tom-tom . . .	Indian drum.
Tulasi . . .	Basil, sacred to Vishnu.
Ugudi . . .	Spring festival.
Upanishads . .	Writings 600 B.C.
Vedas . . .	Sacred hymns 1,500 B.C.
Vina . . .	Musical instrument.
Vythian . . .	Doctor.
Wallah . . .	Suffix meaning "One who is."
Yaga . . .	Animal sacrifice.
Zemindar . . .	Landowner, chief.
Zenana . . .	Women's apartments.

INDEX